Edvard Grieg
23 Little Piano Pieces
EG104

Transcribed by Irina Maslakova

Original manuscript provided by Edvard Grieg's Archive and Collection
hosted by the Bergen Public Library.

ISBN 978-1-326-96637-9

Cover art by freepik.com

conspirito

Edvard Grieg
23 Little Piano Pieces EG104
(1858-1859)

CONTENTS

ISBN 978-1-326-96637-9

23 Little Piano Pieces

1.

Edvard Grieg, EG 104
1858-1859

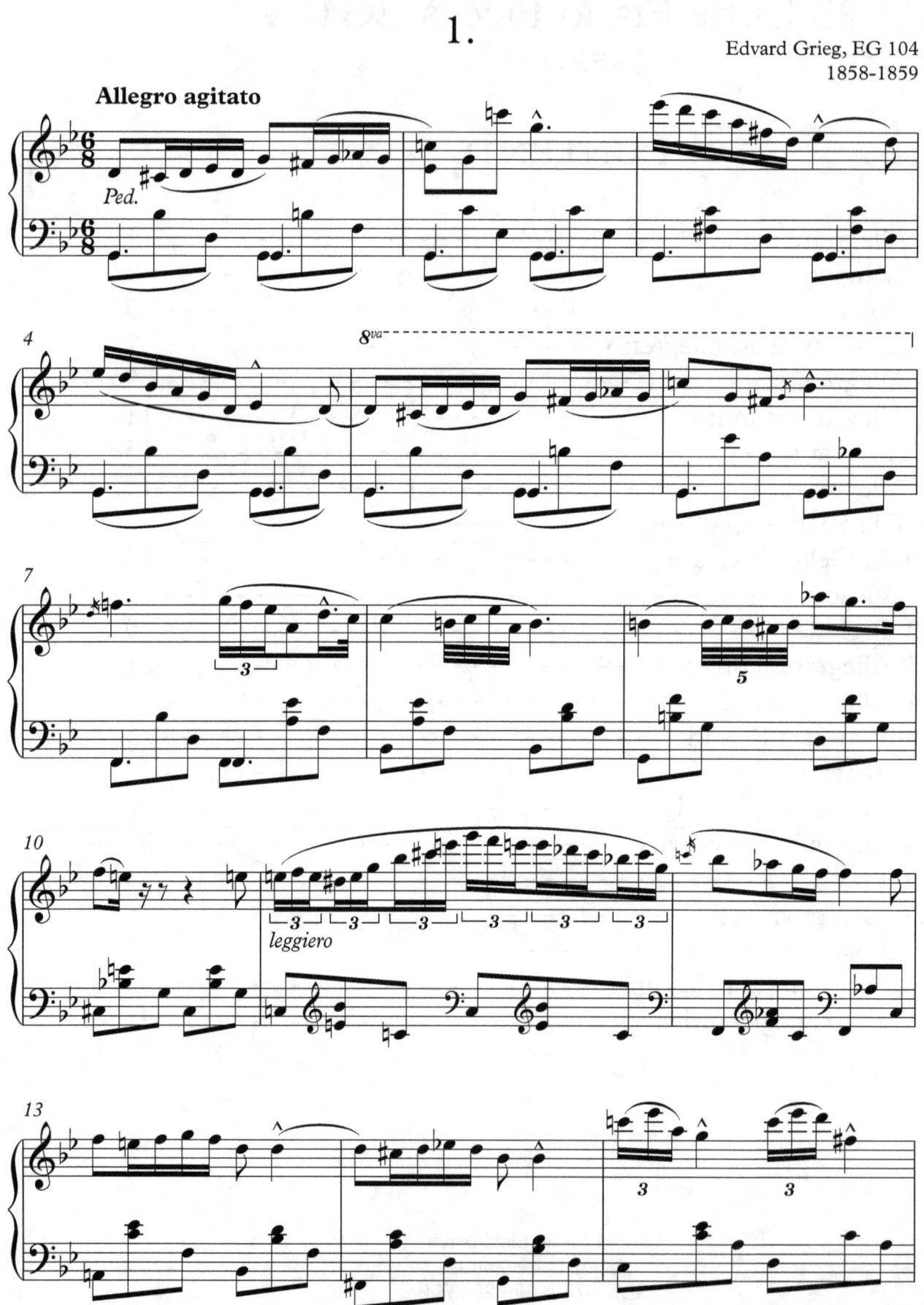

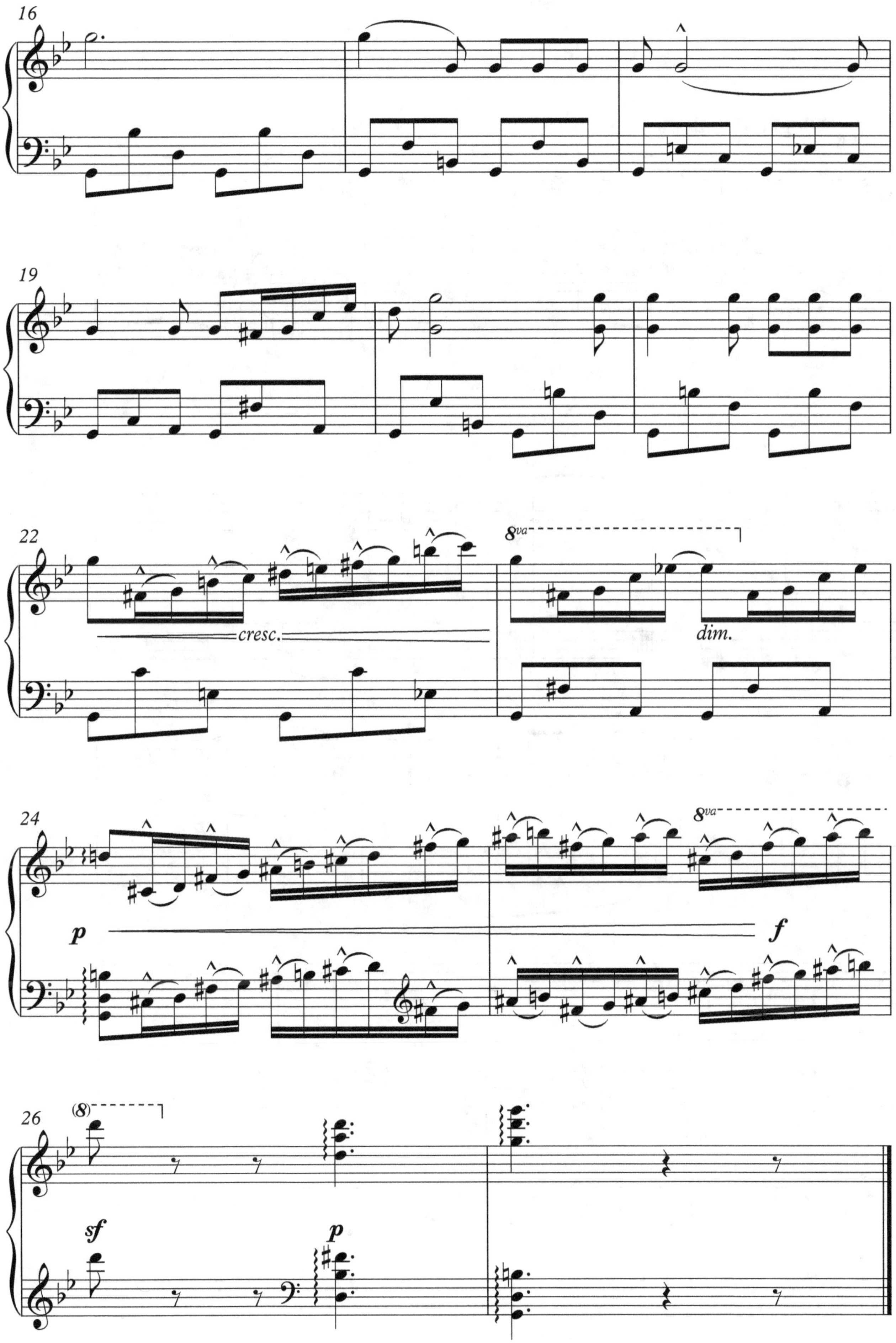

2.

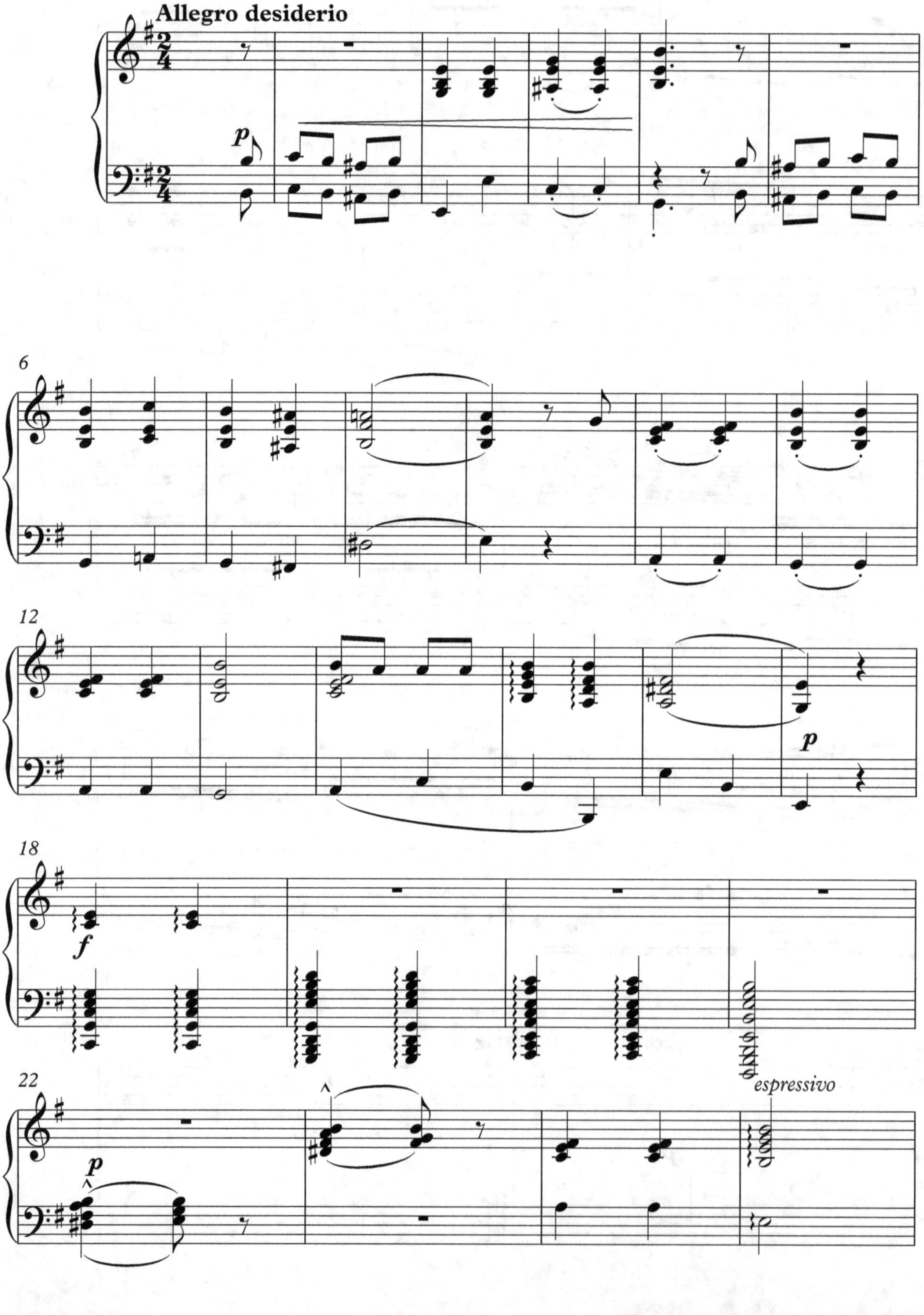

Allegro desiderio

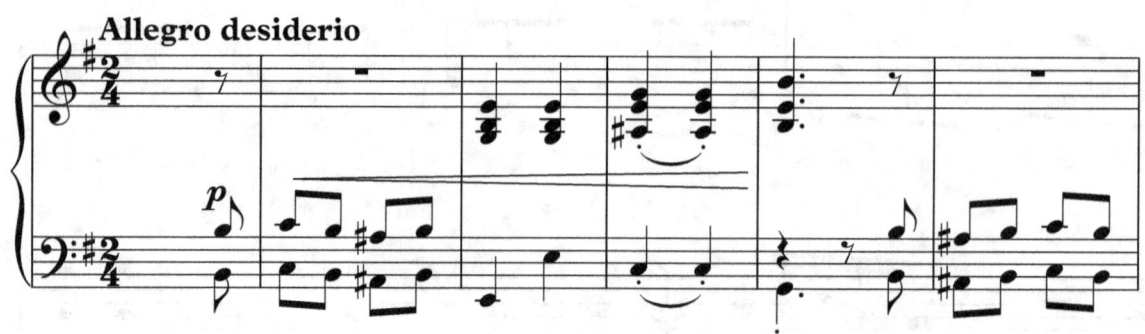

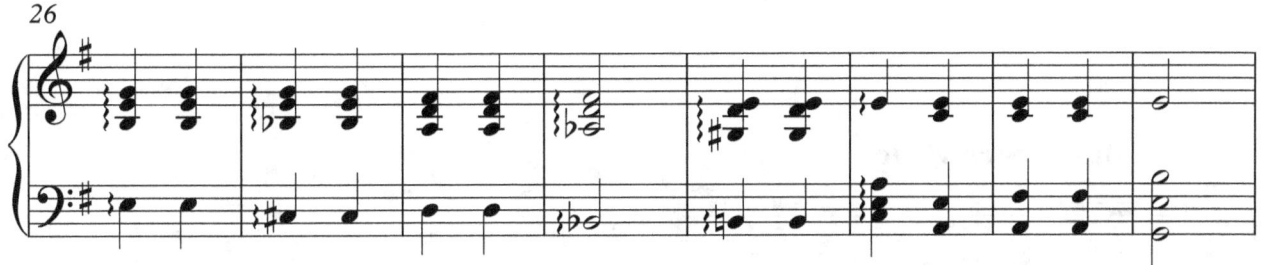

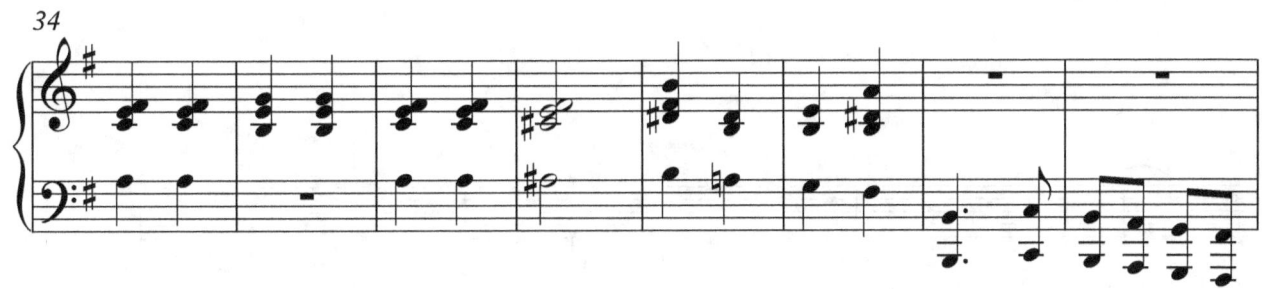

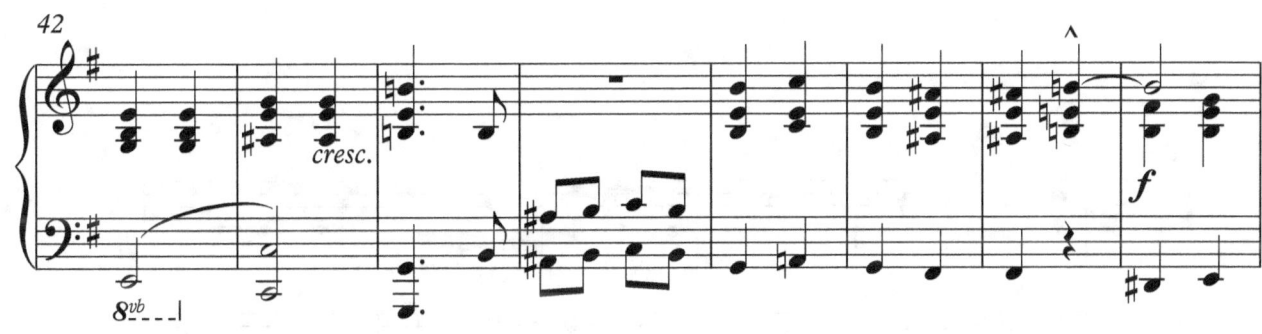

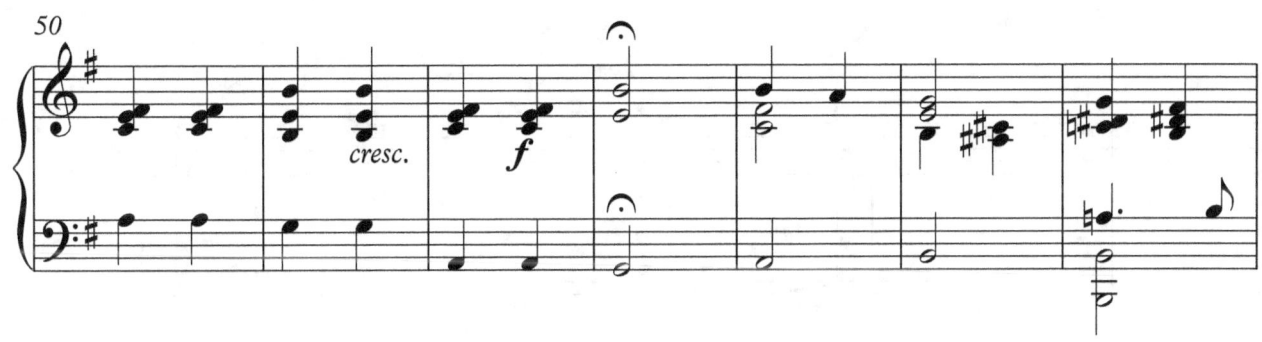

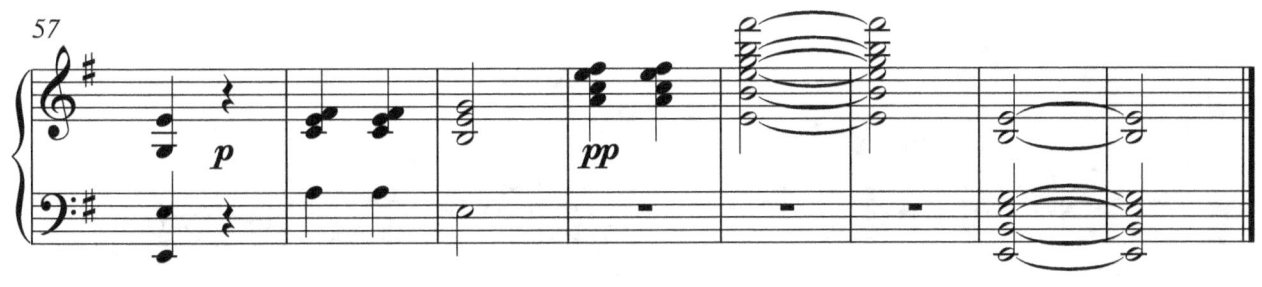

3. Scherzo

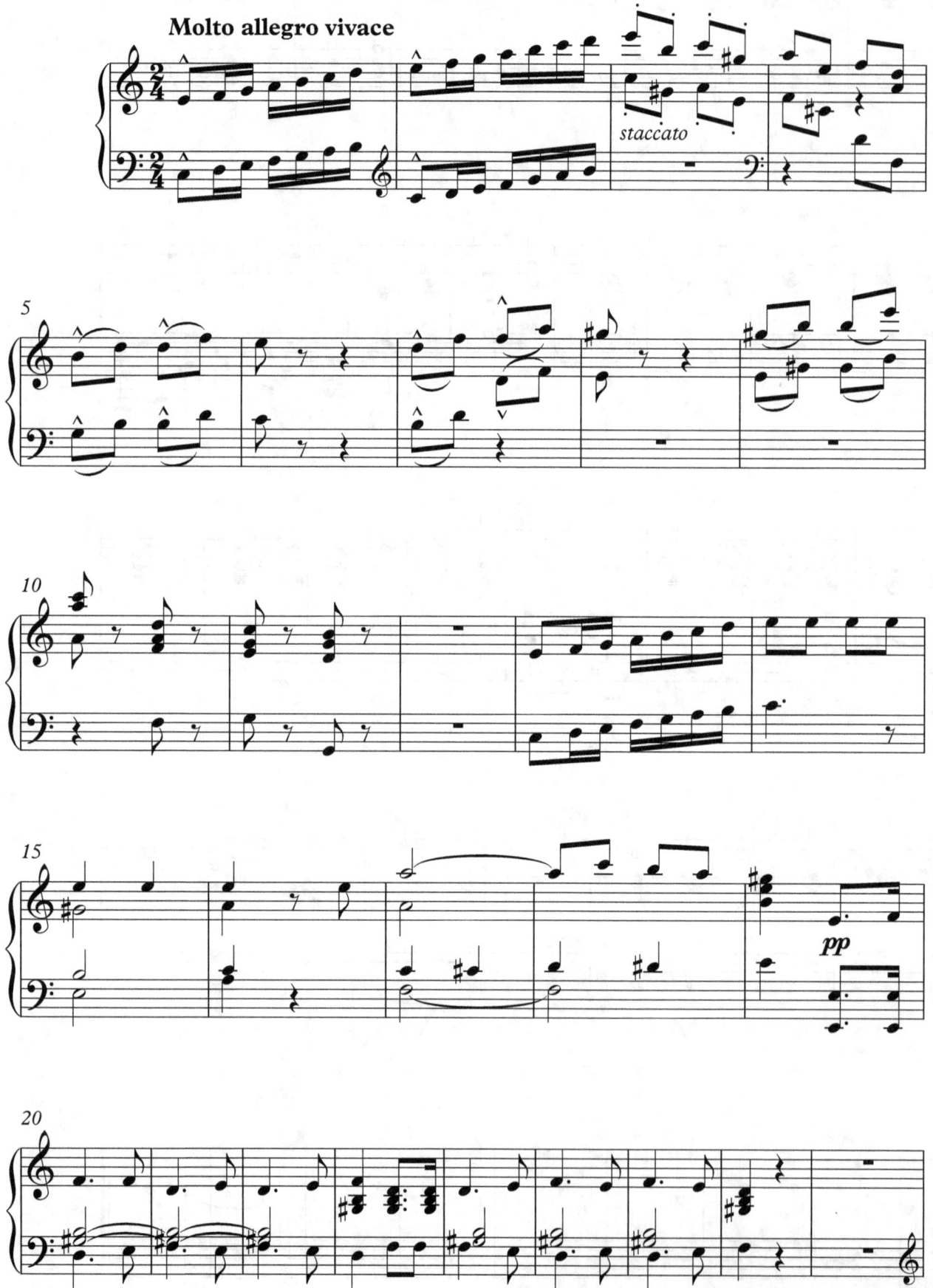

6

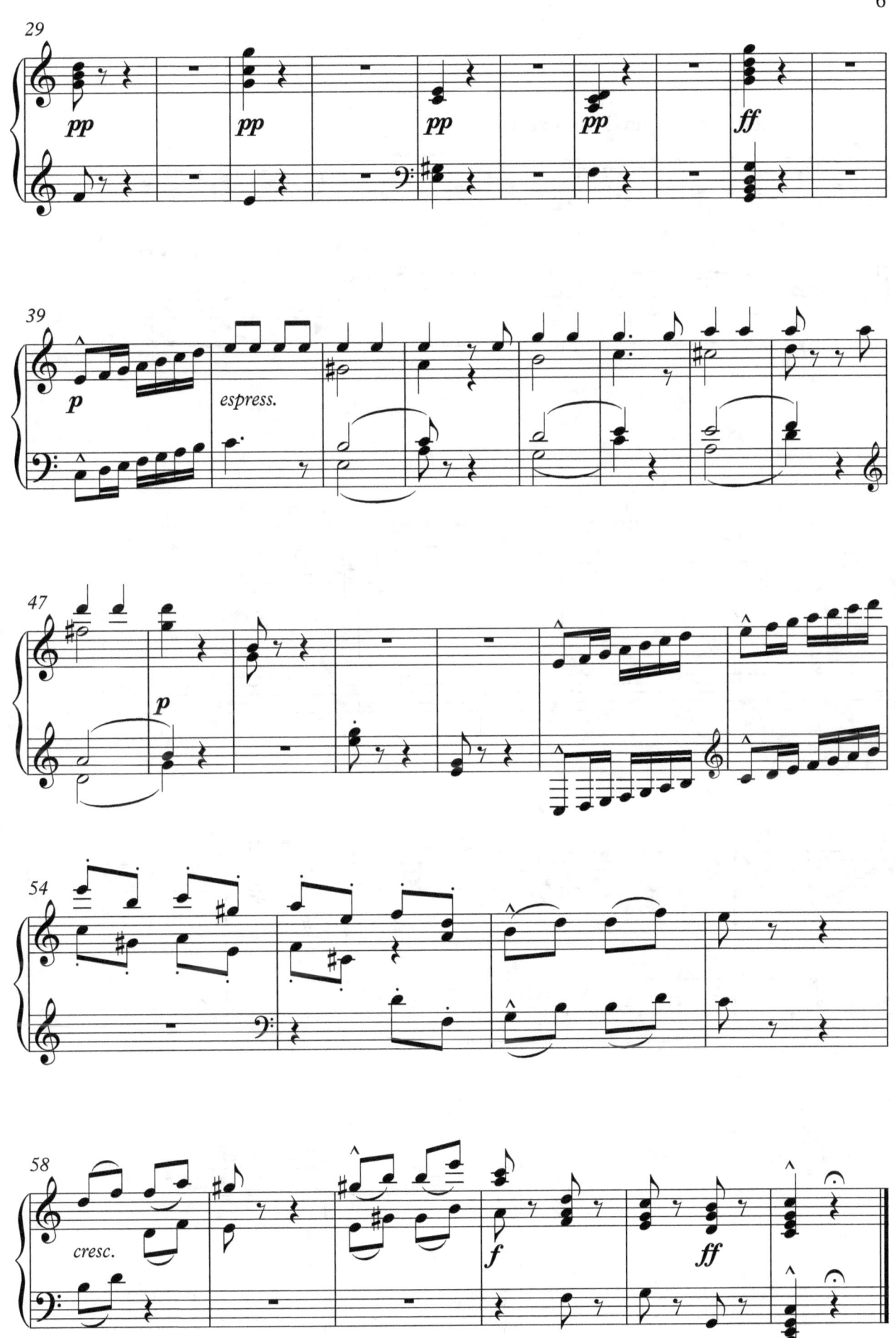

4.

Andante, quasi allegretto

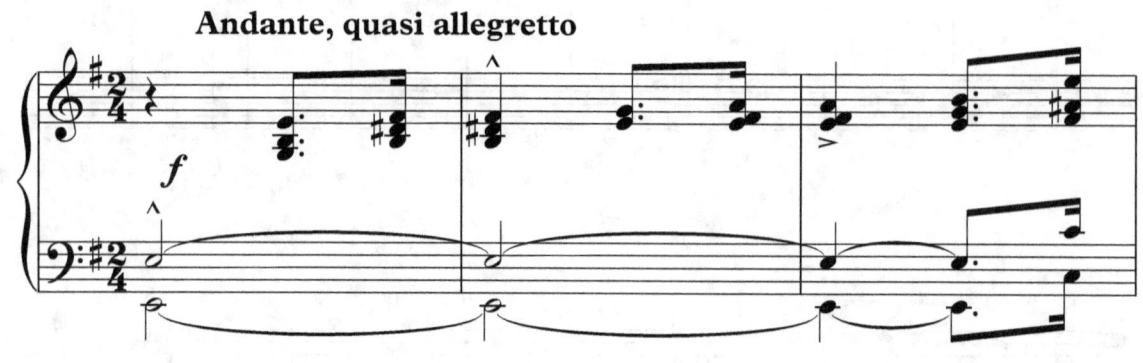

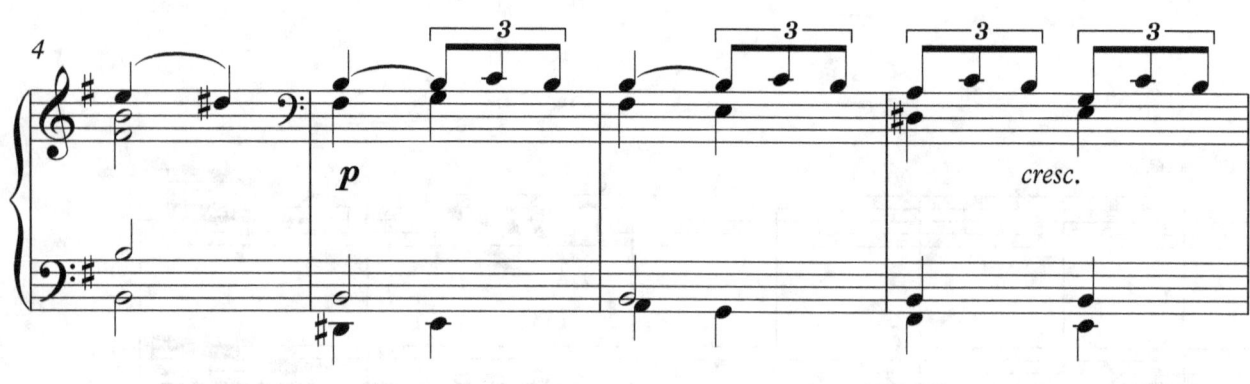

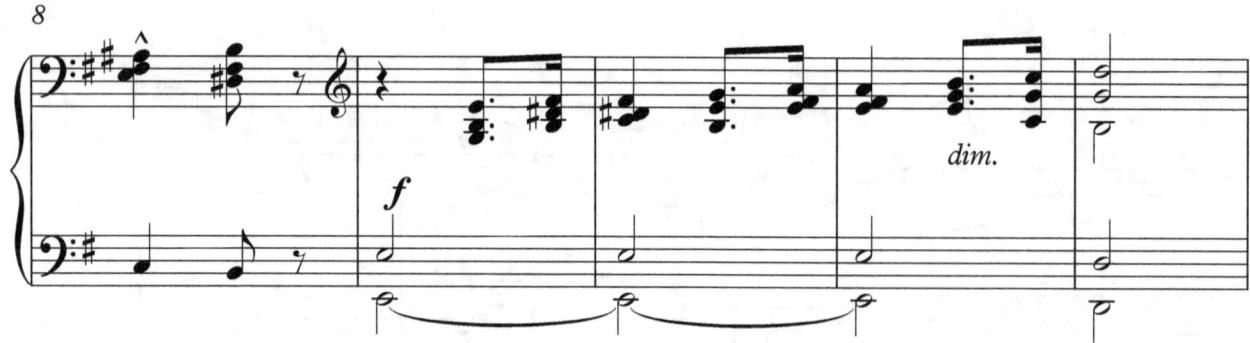

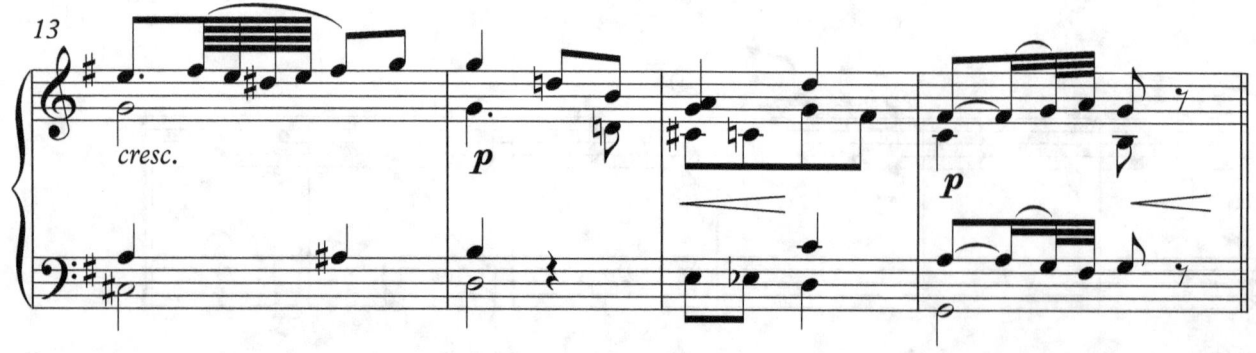

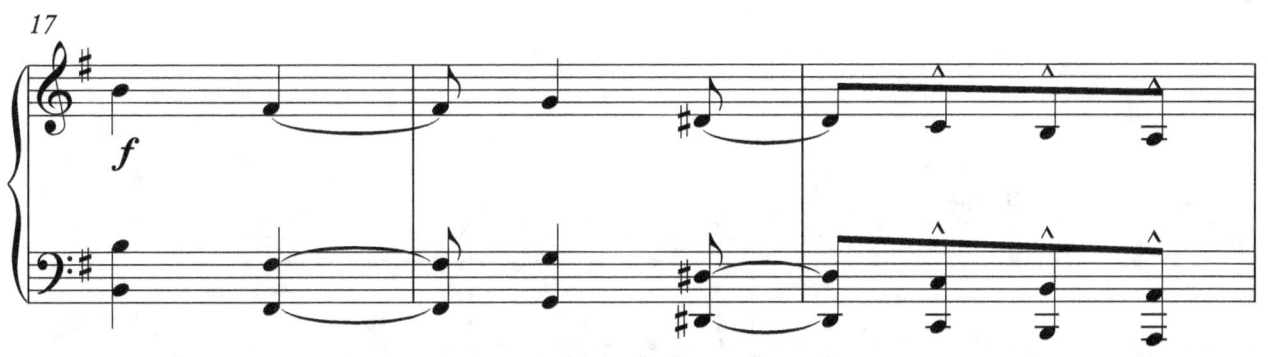

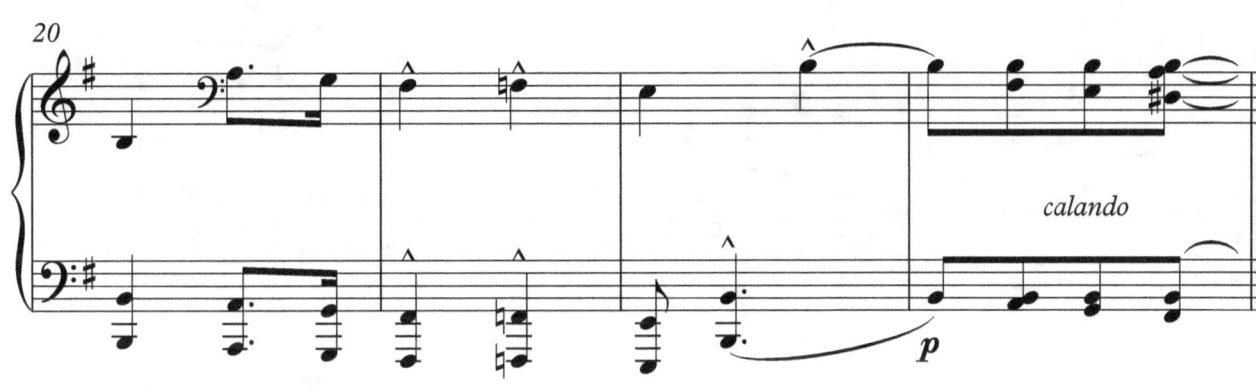

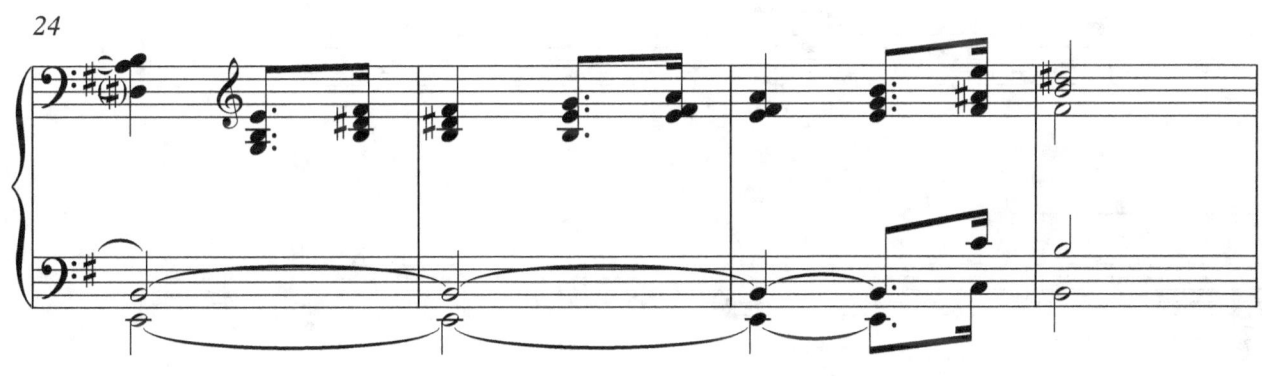

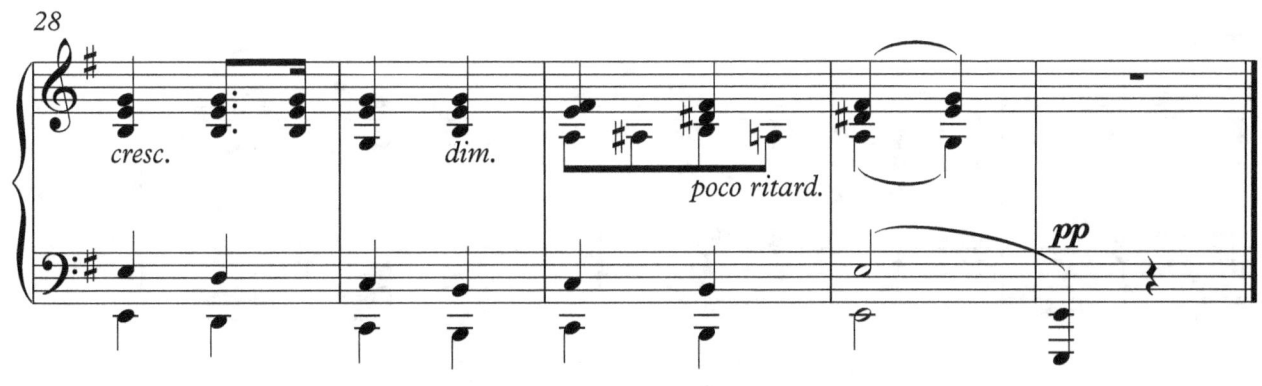

5.

Allegro assai

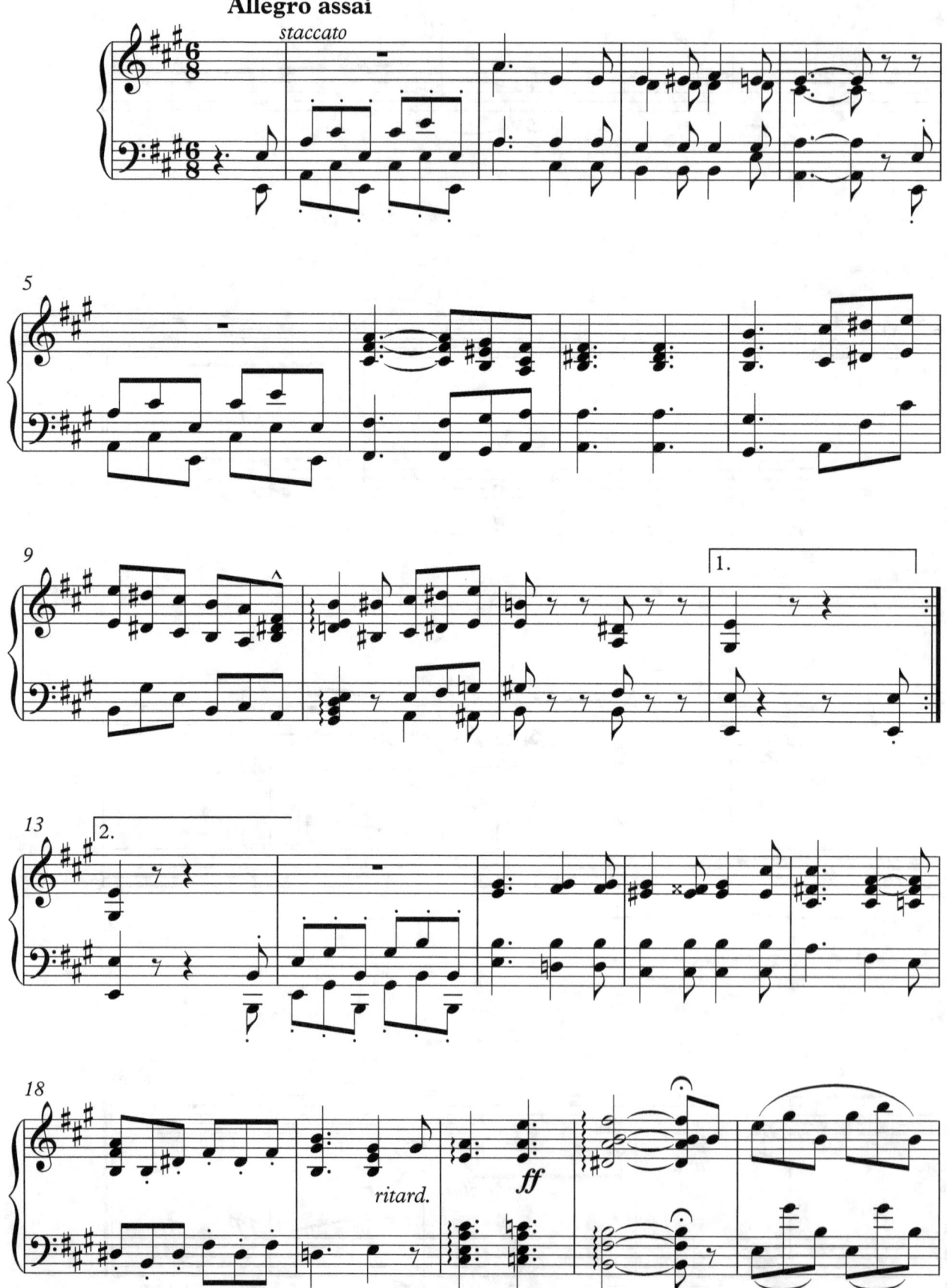

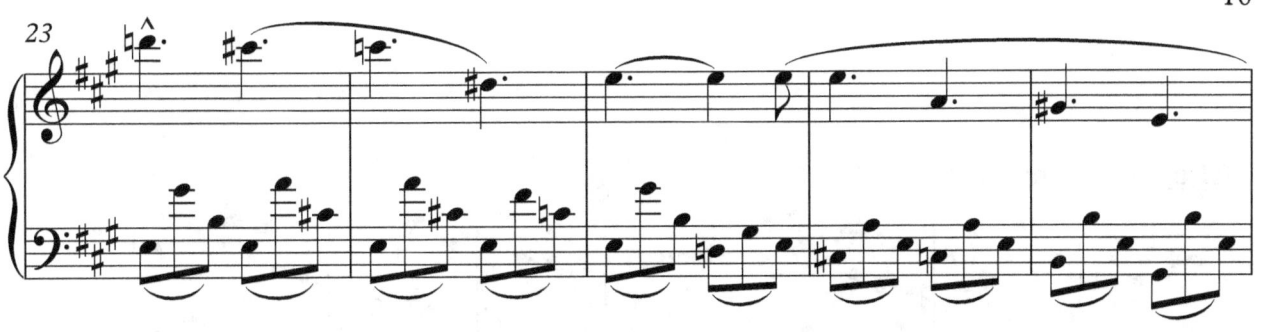

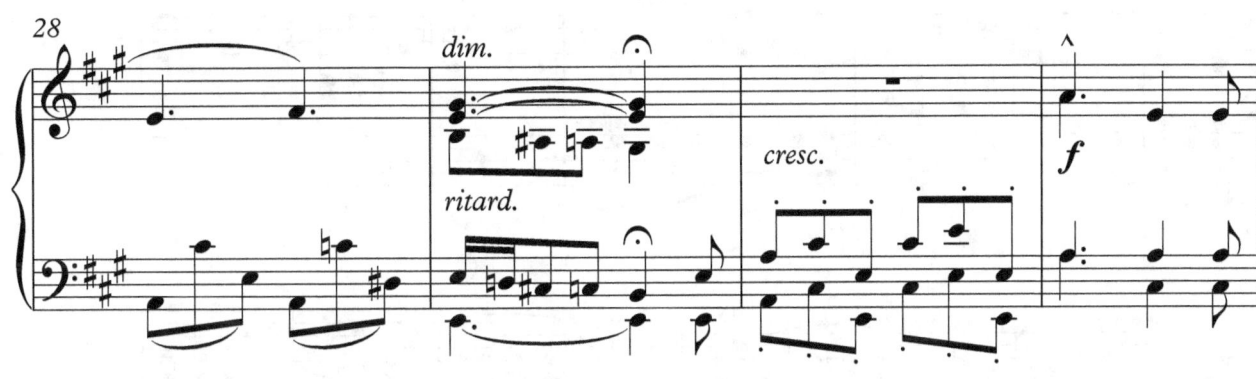

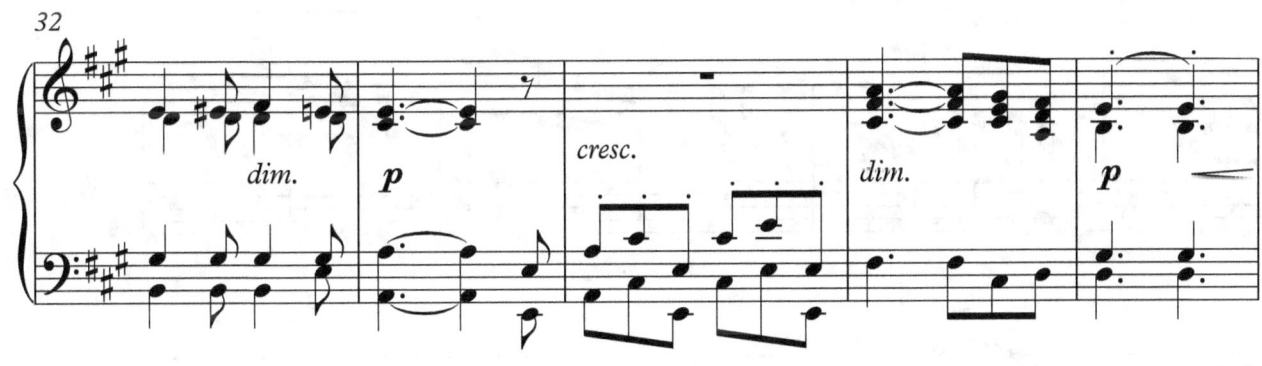

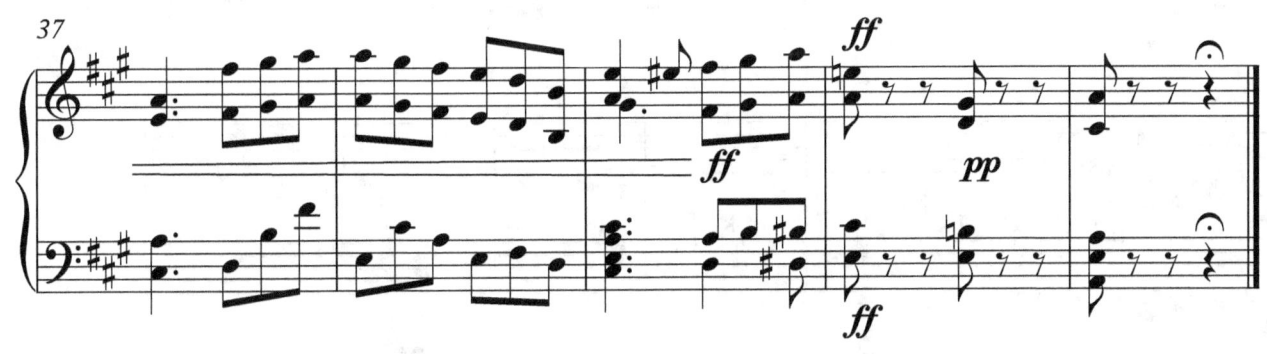

6.

Allegro con moto

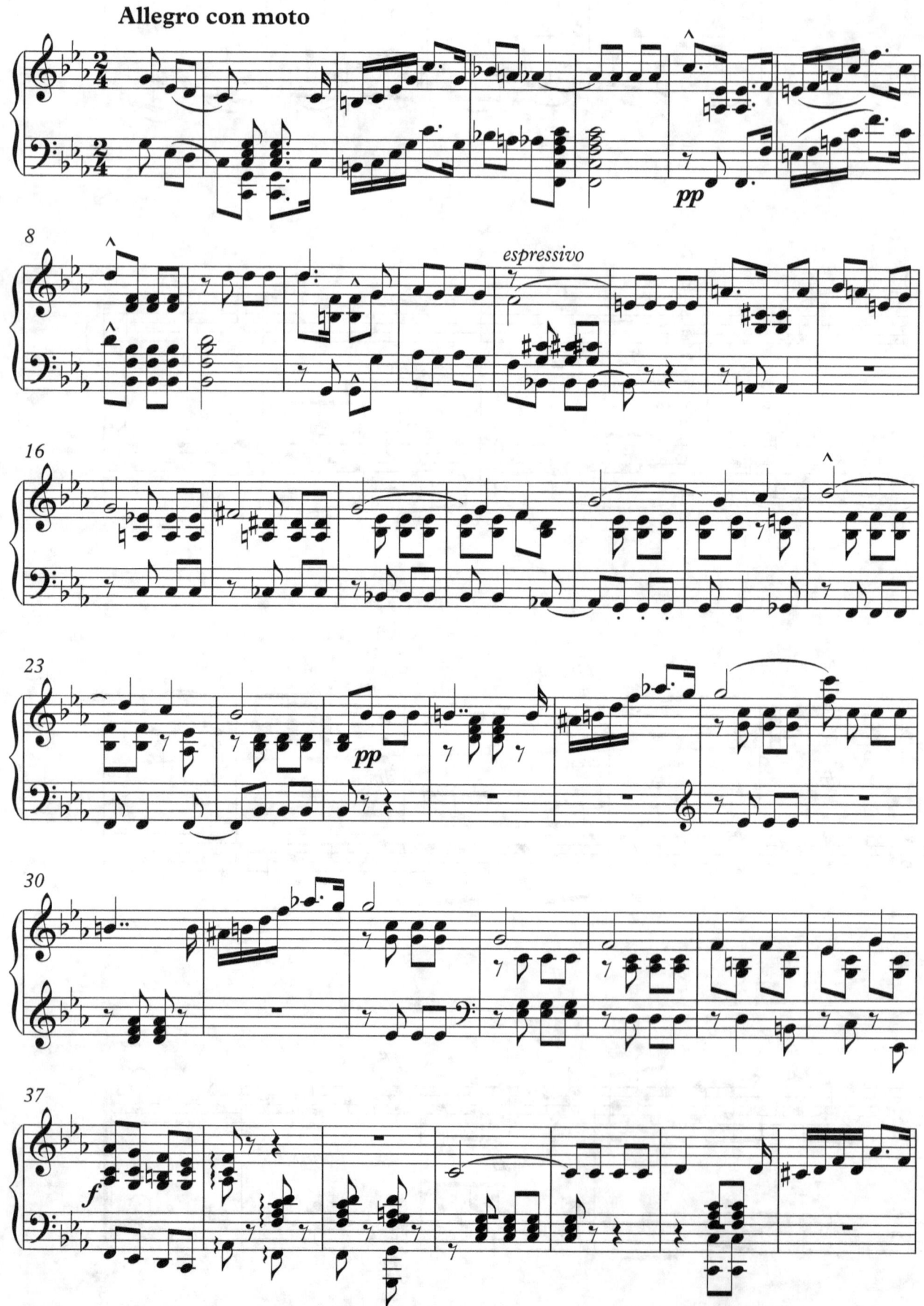

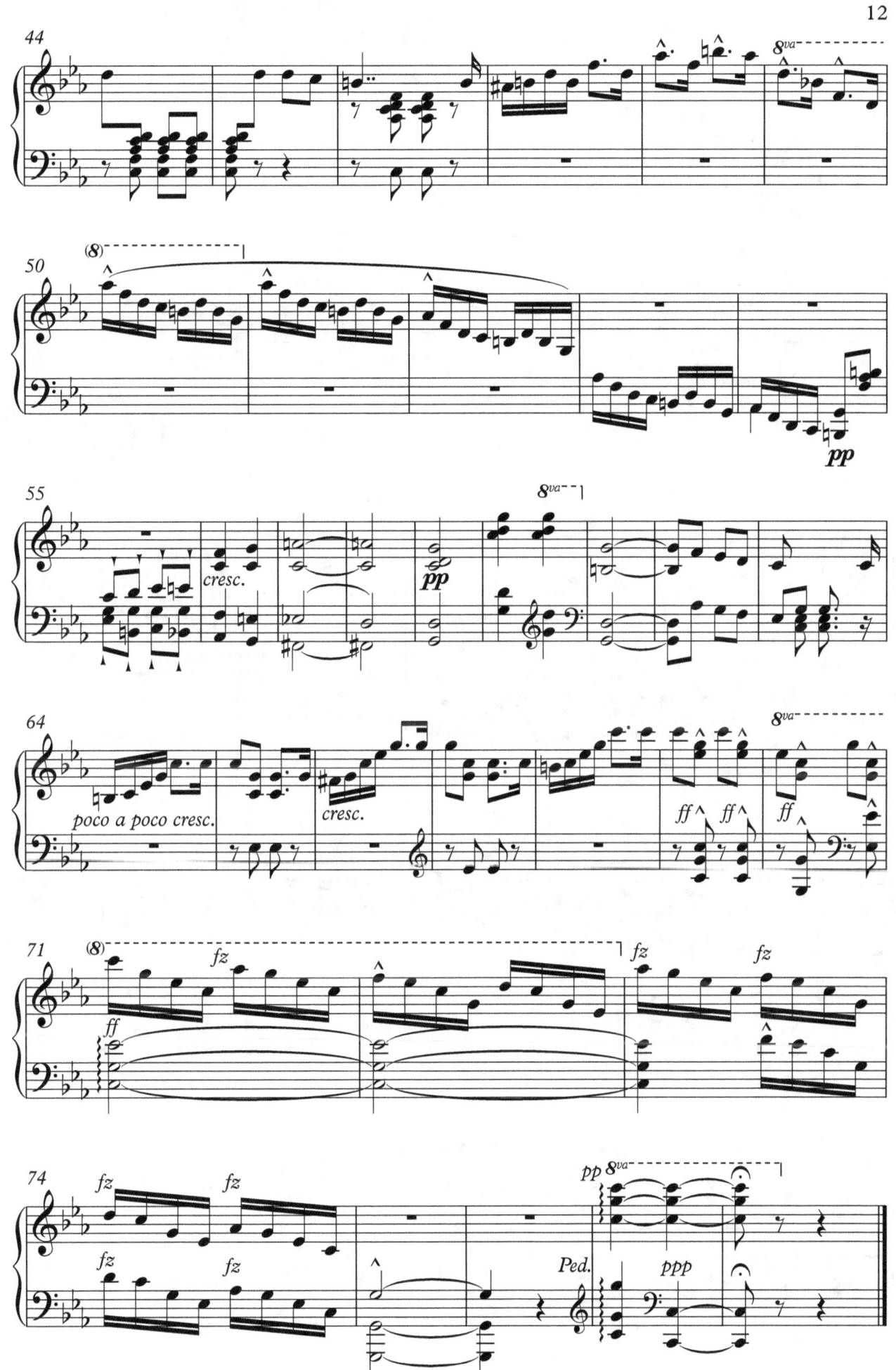

7.

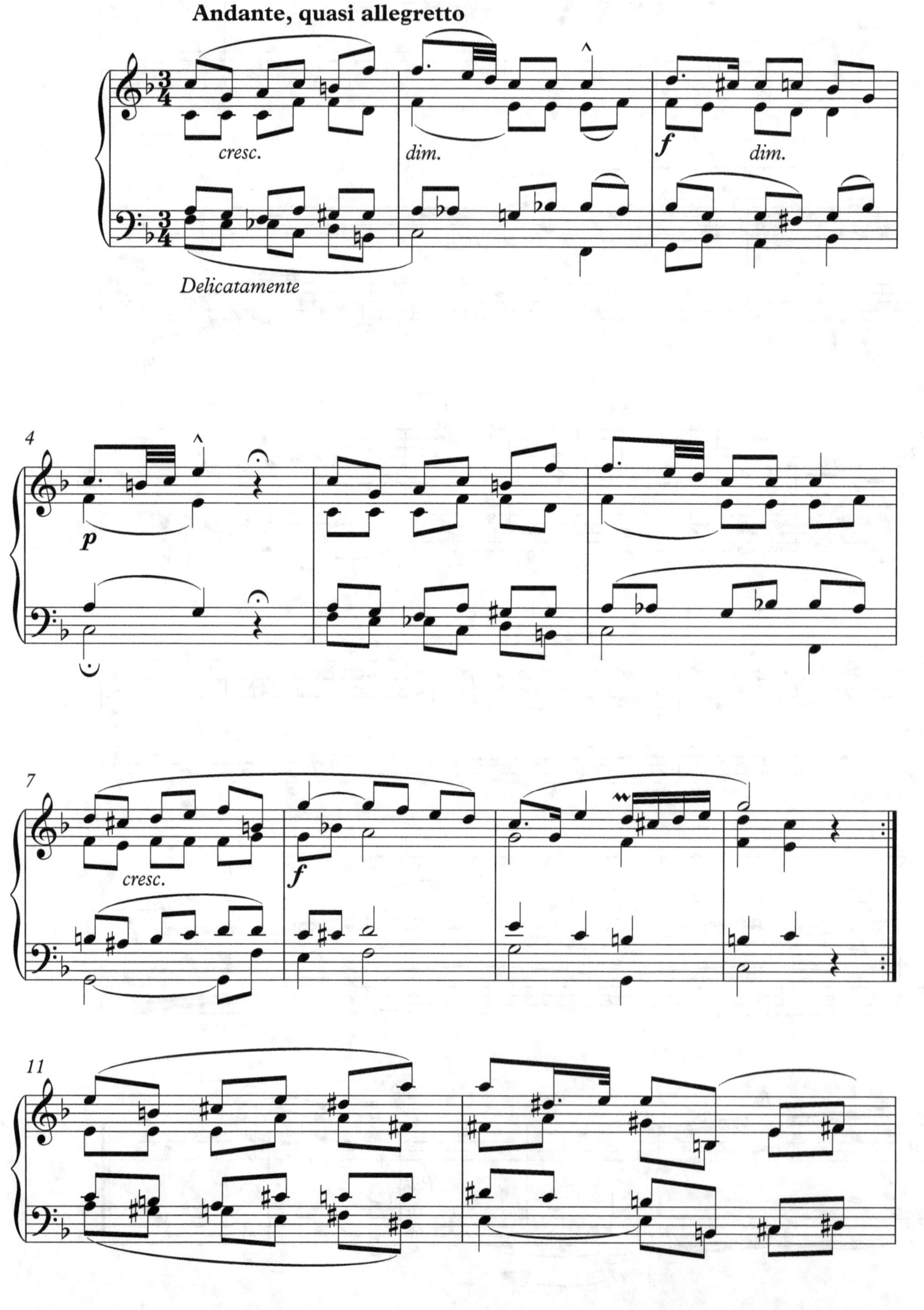

Andante, quasi allegretto

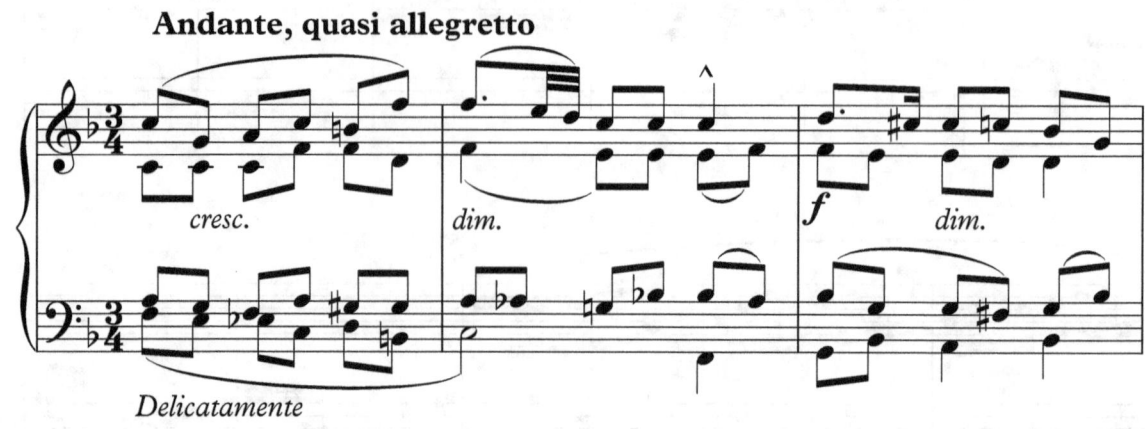

poco a poco rallentando

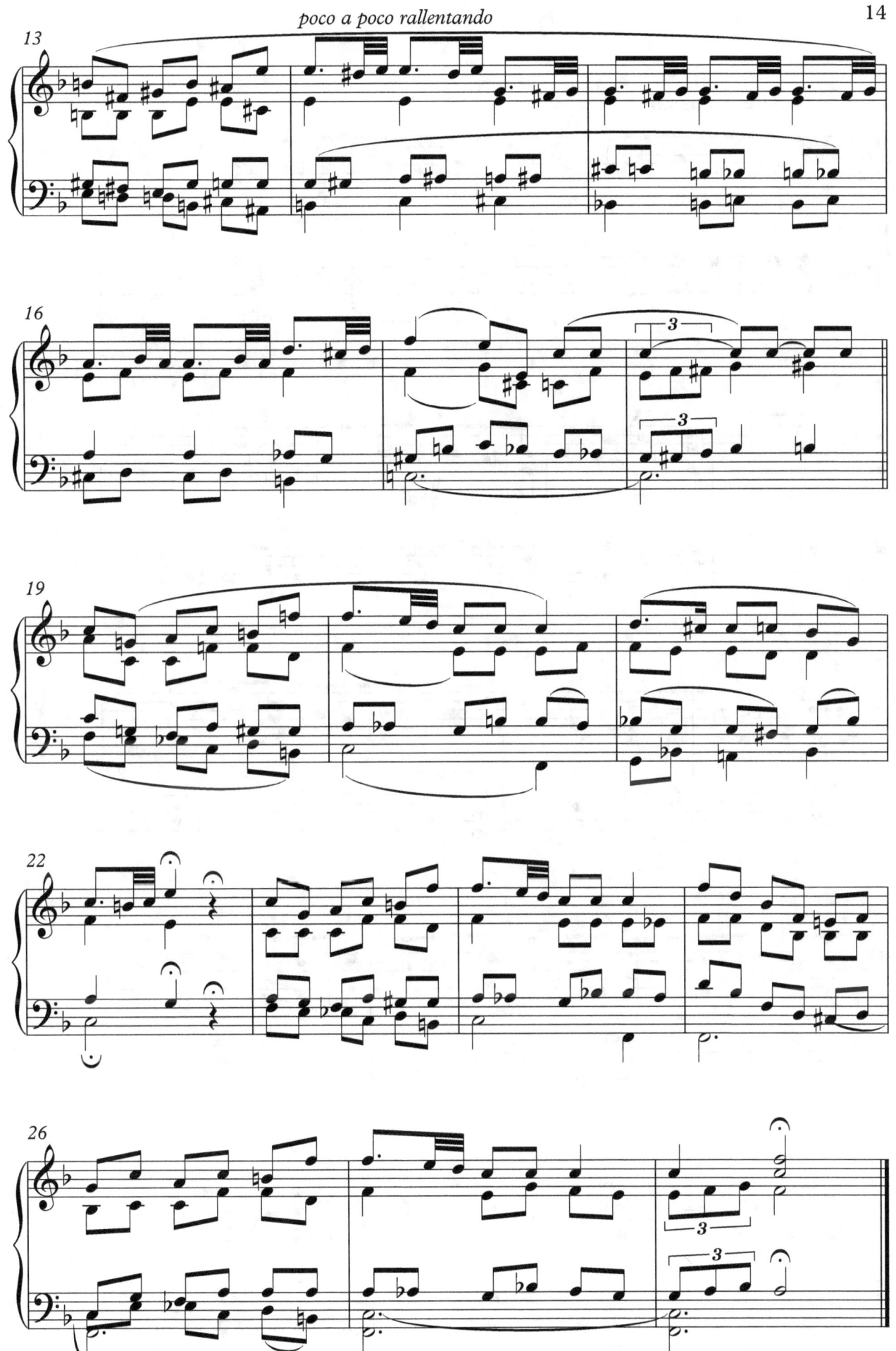

8.

Allegro assai

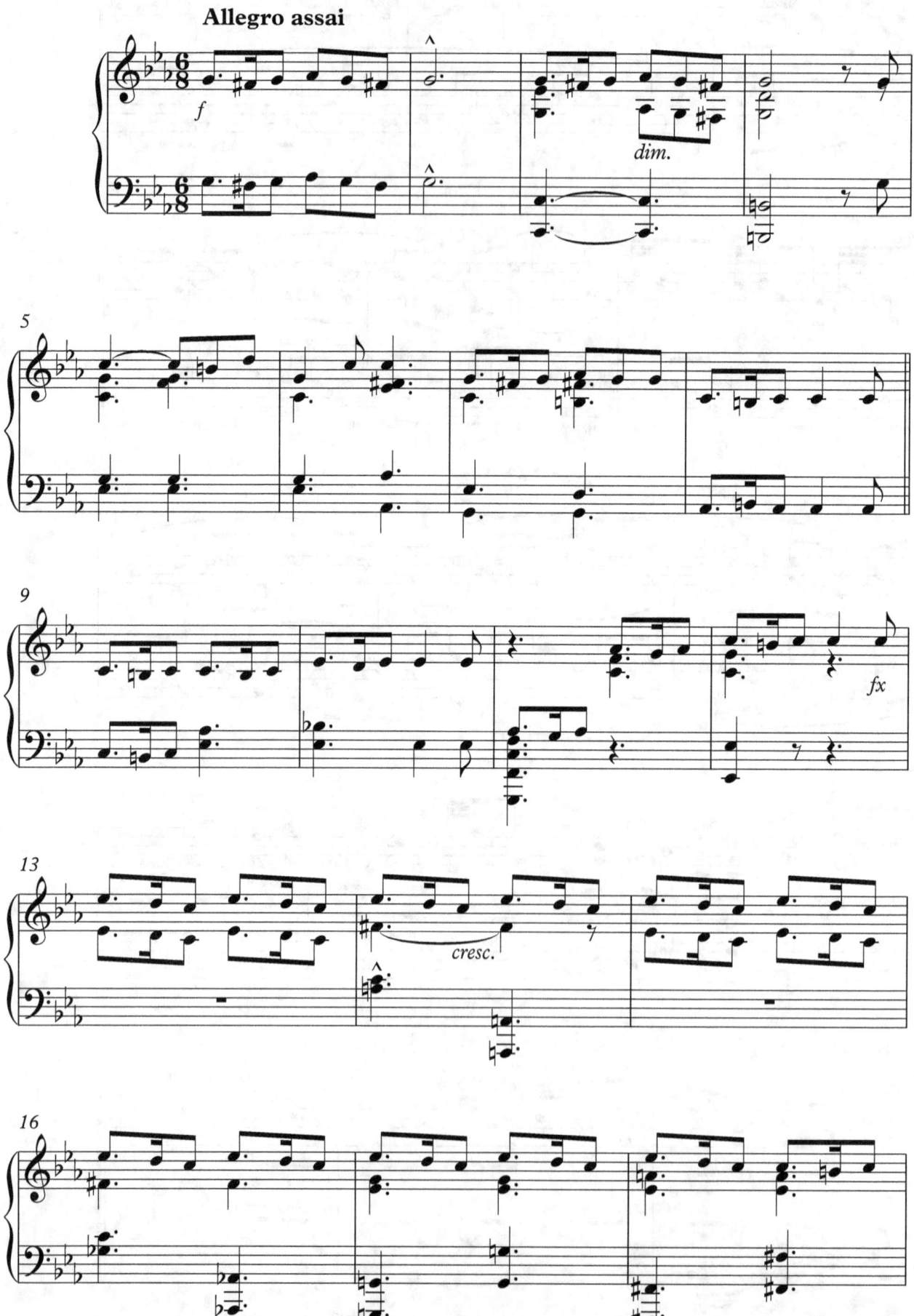

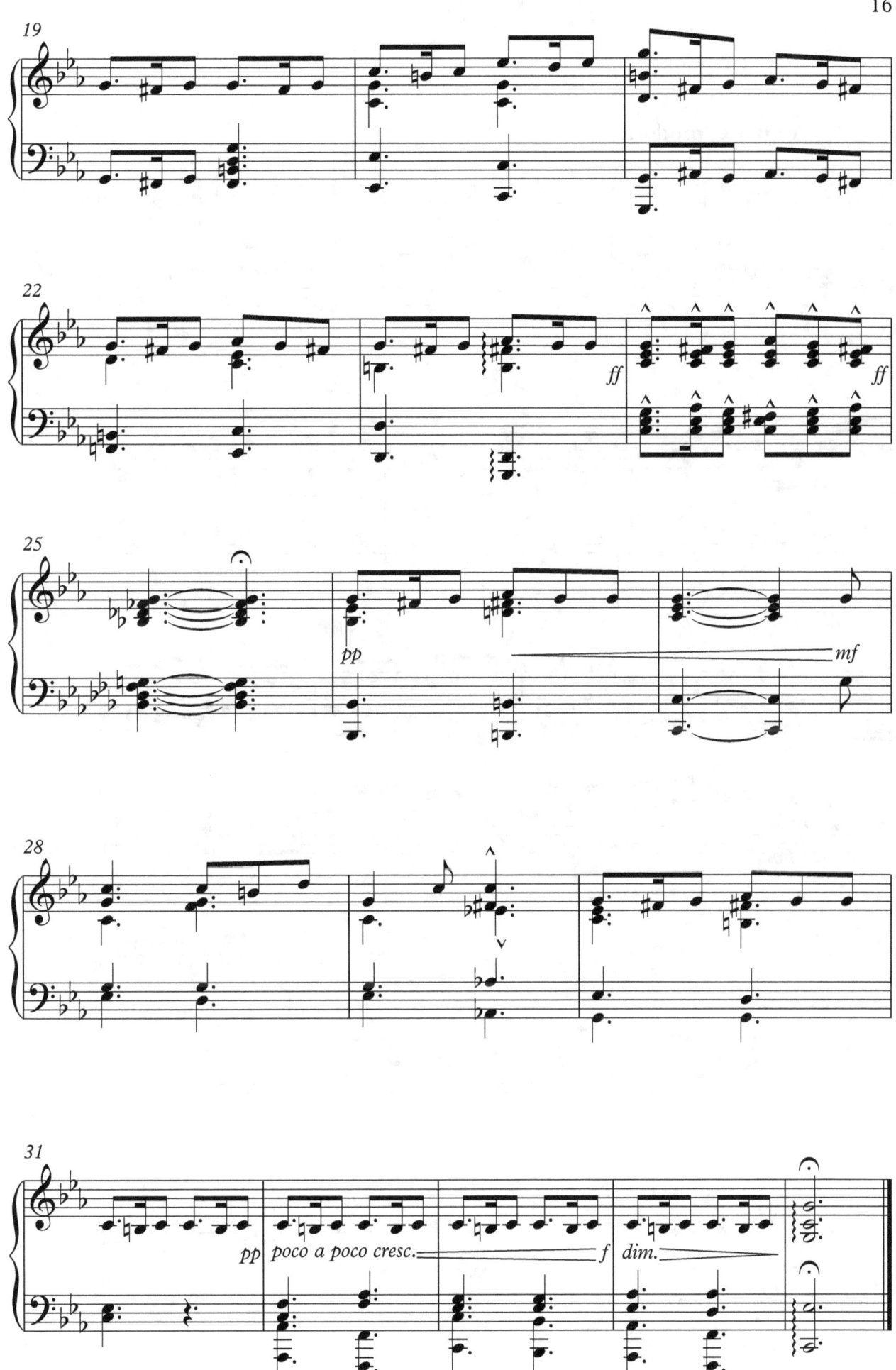

17

9. The Pearl

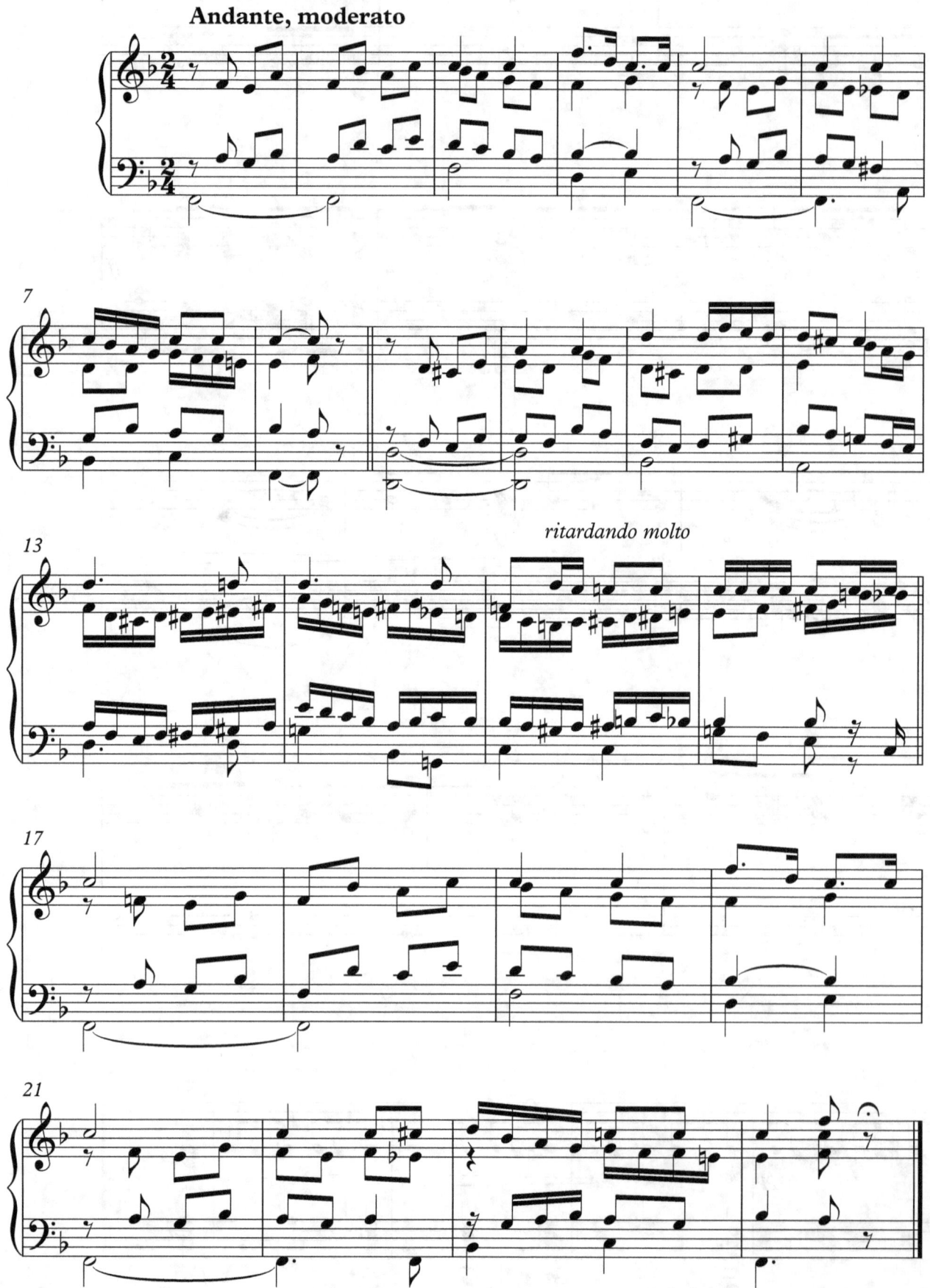

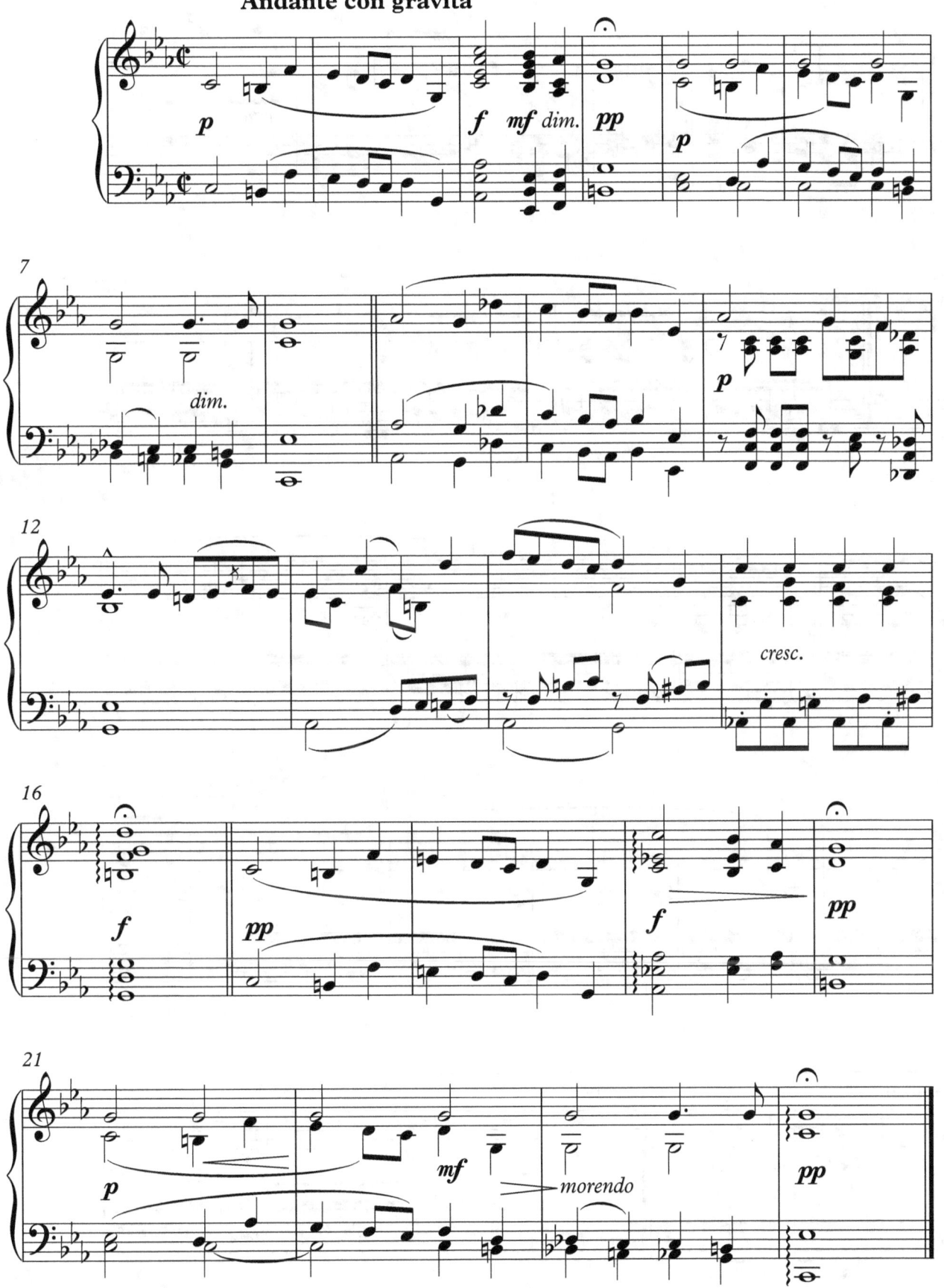

10.

Andante con gravita

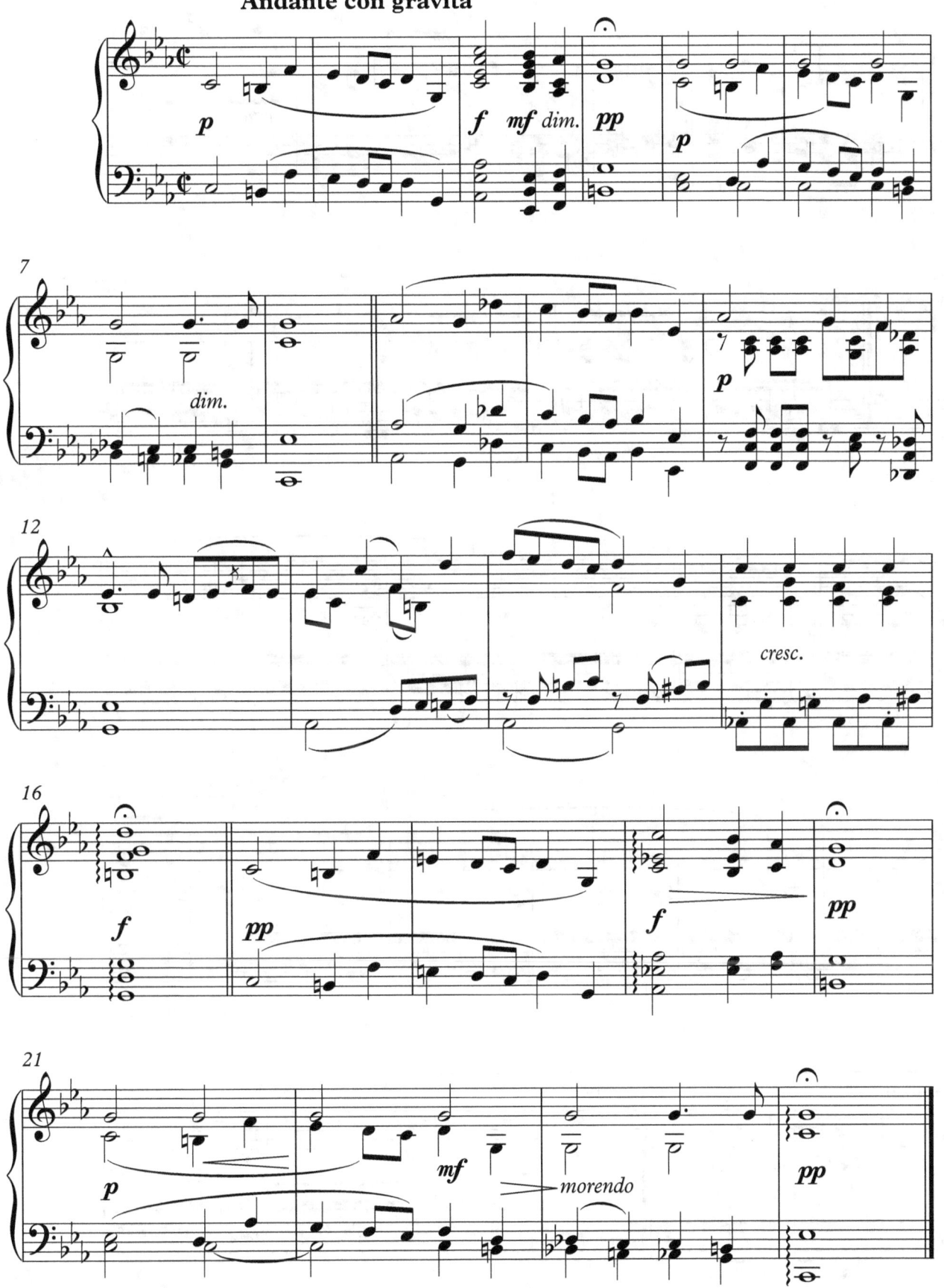

11.

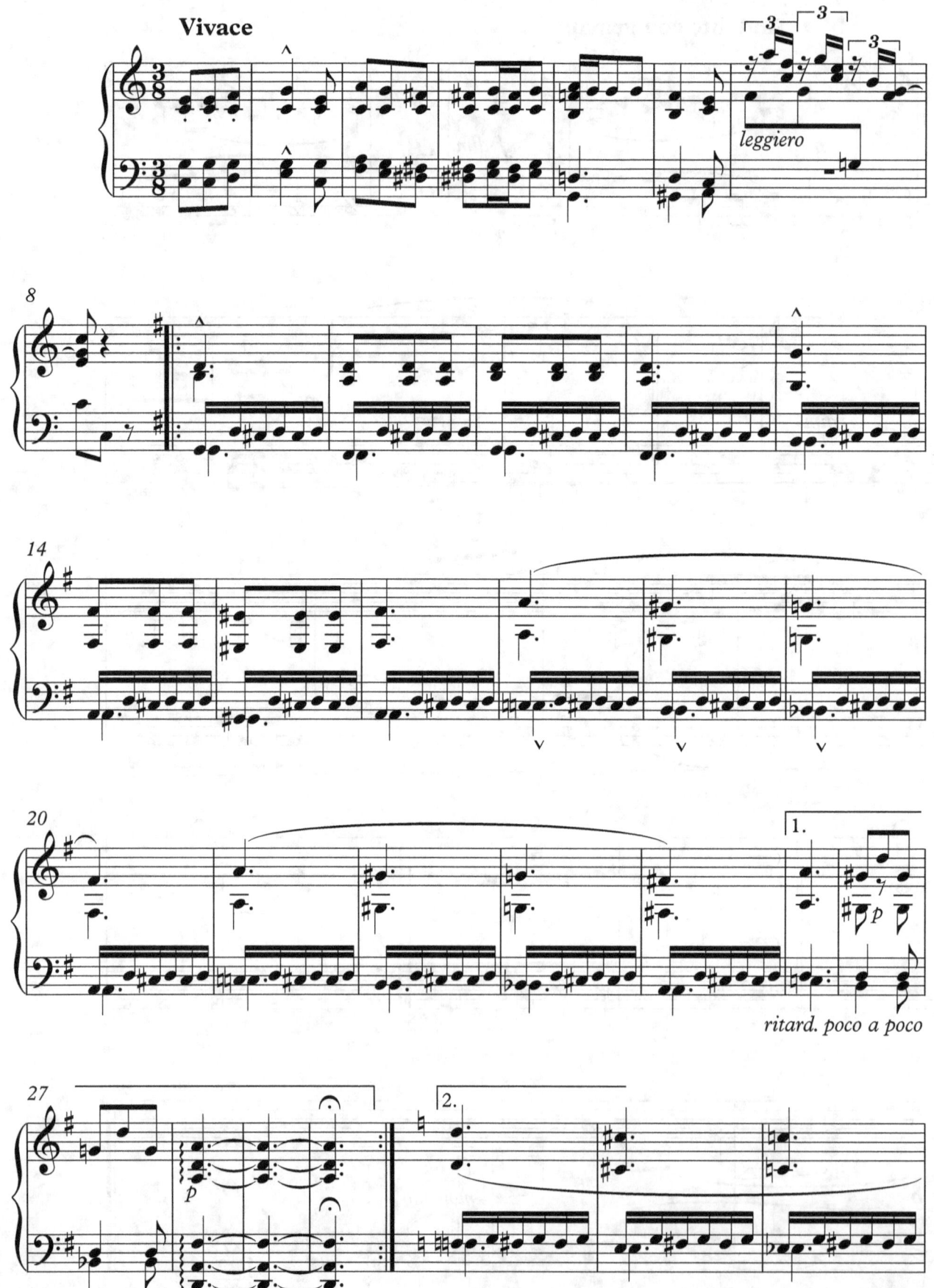

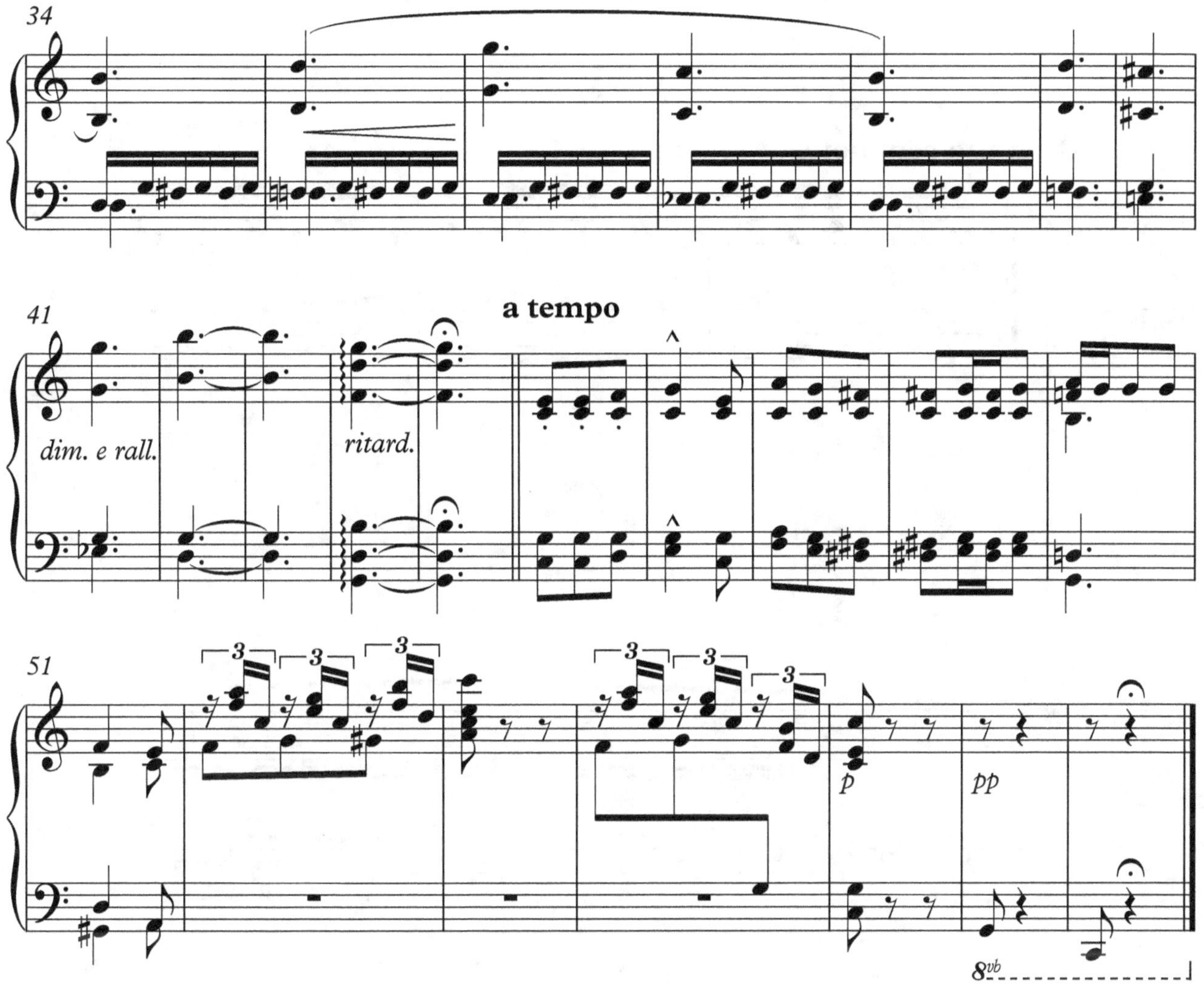

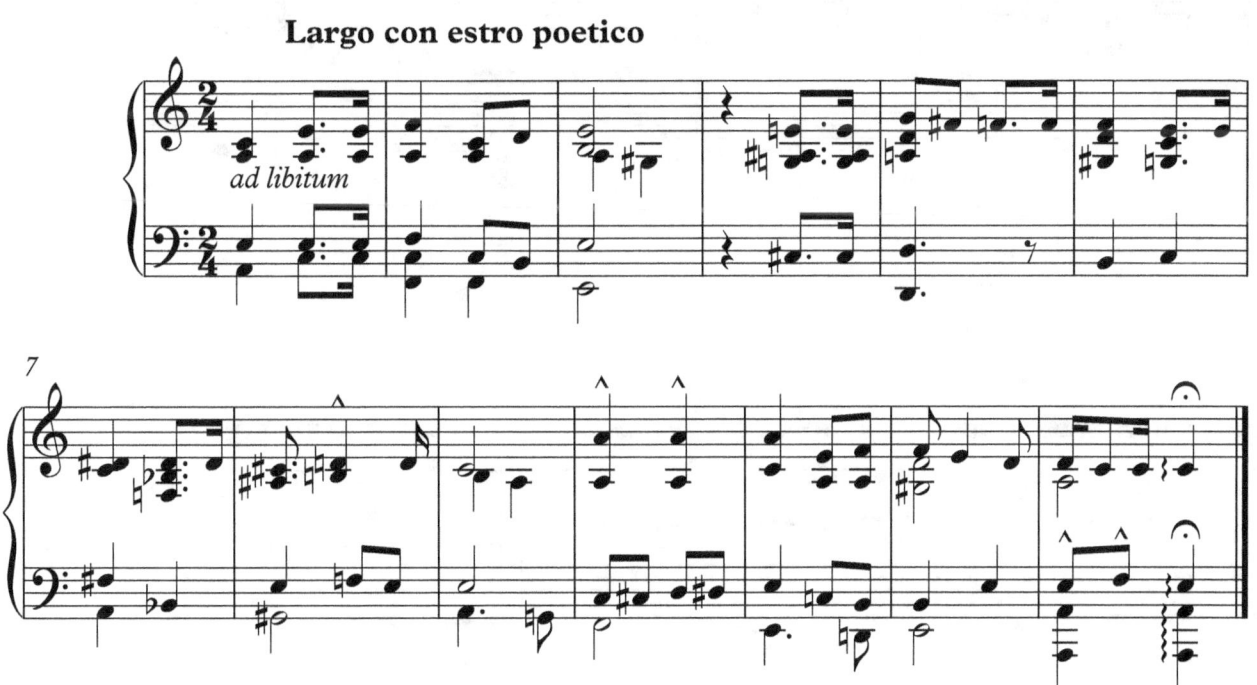

12. Prelude

13.

Allegretto con moto

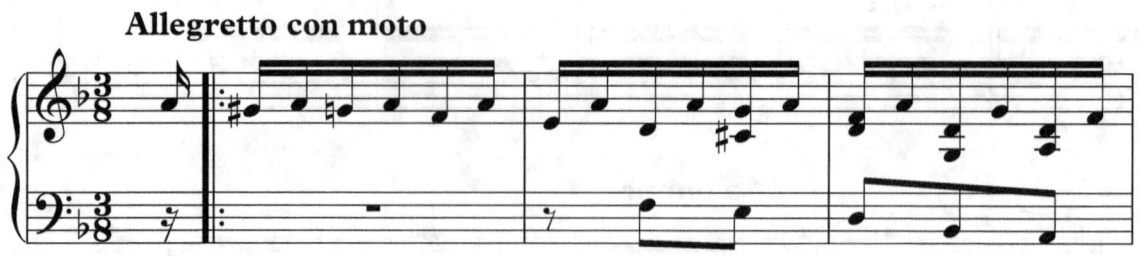

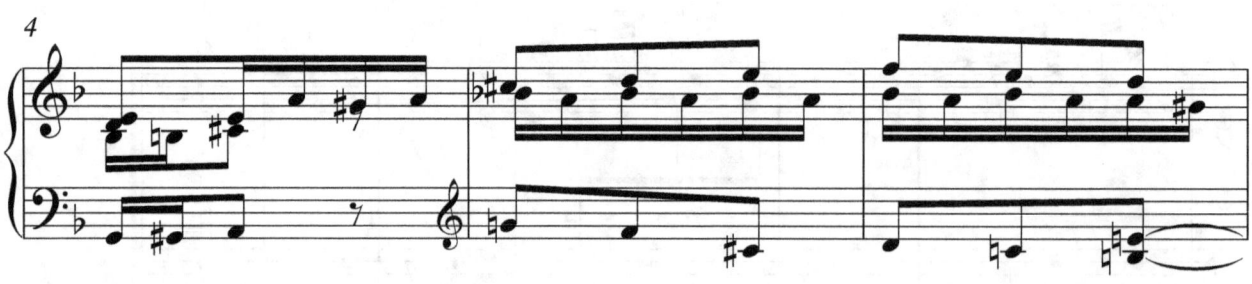

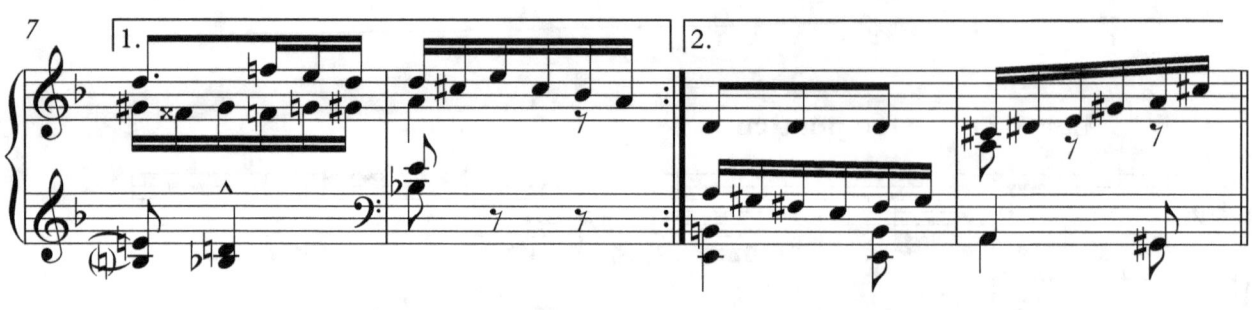

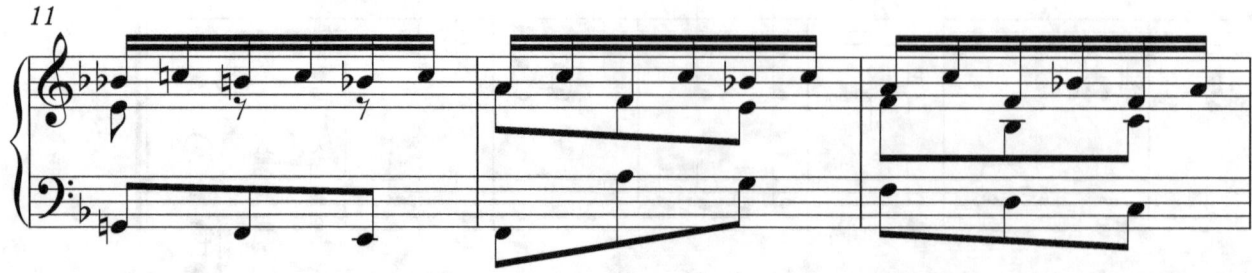

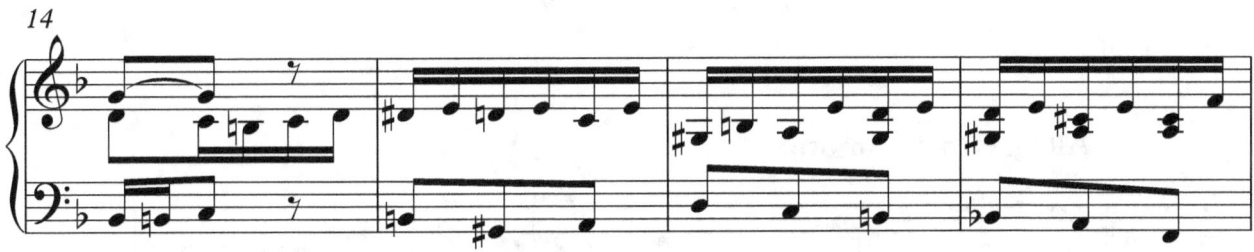

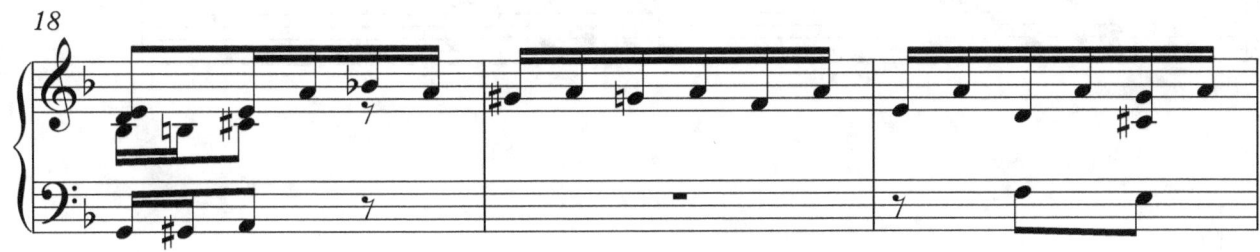

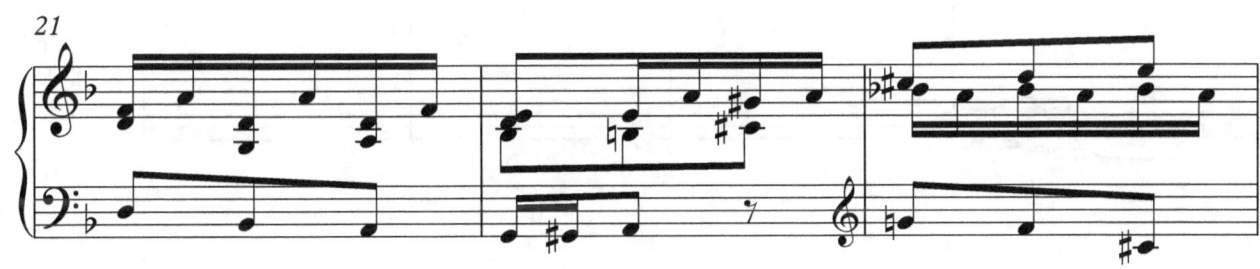

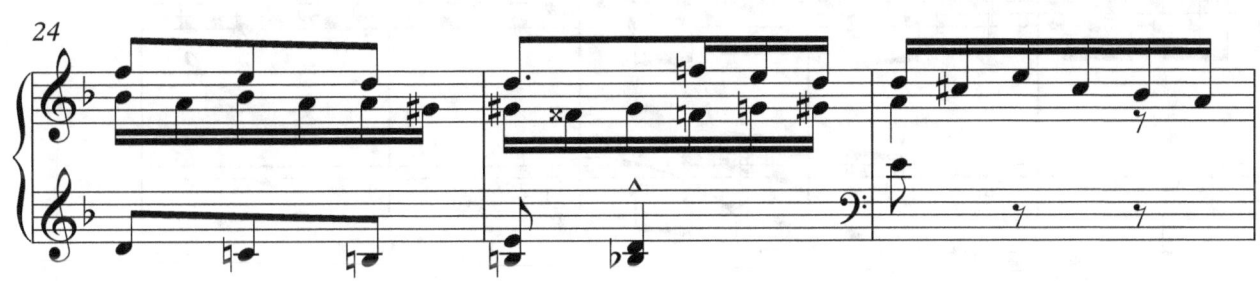

poco a poco dim. e ritard.

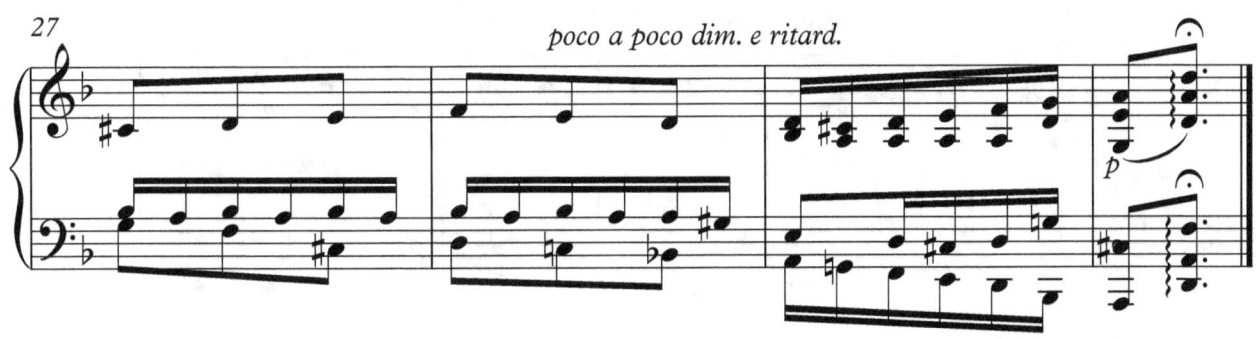

14.

Allegretto con moto

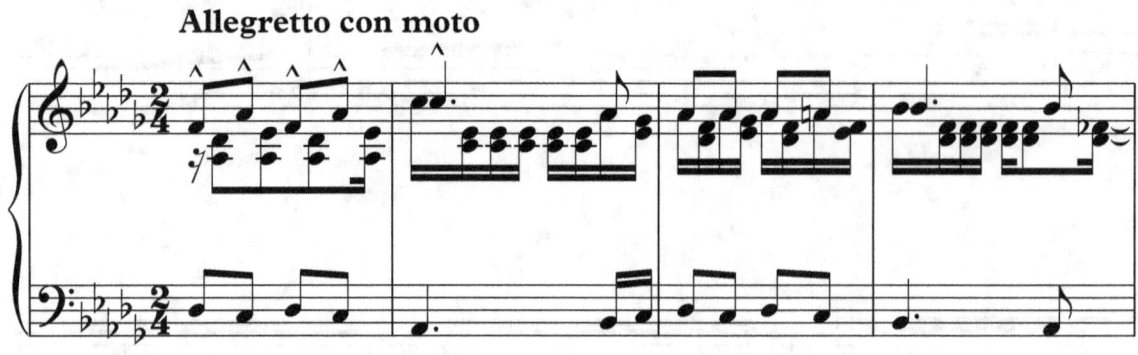

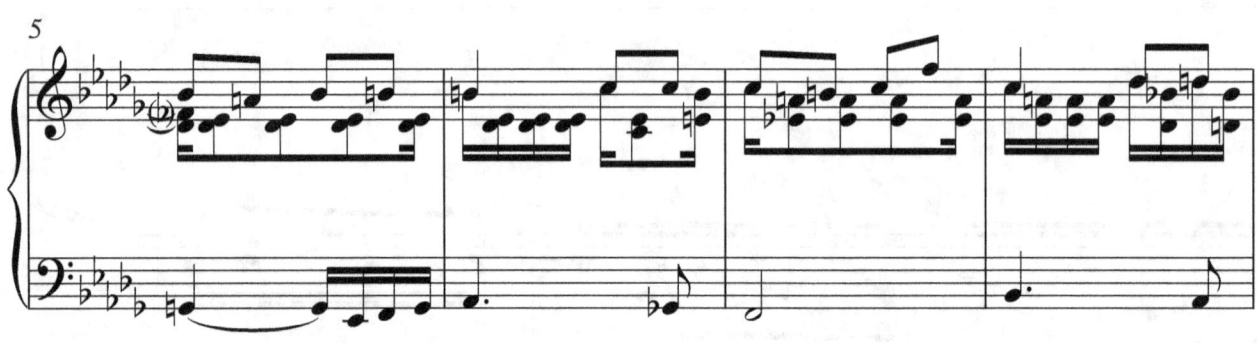

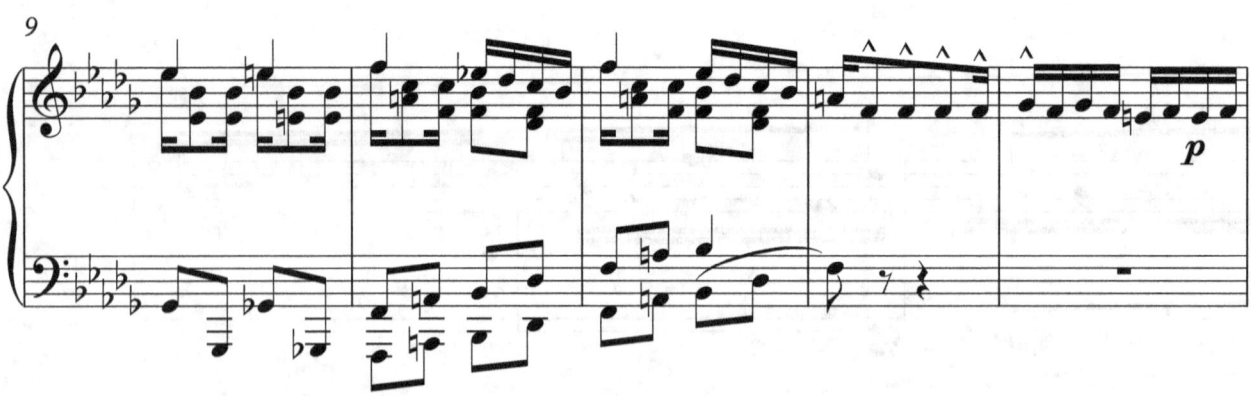

poco a poco ritard.

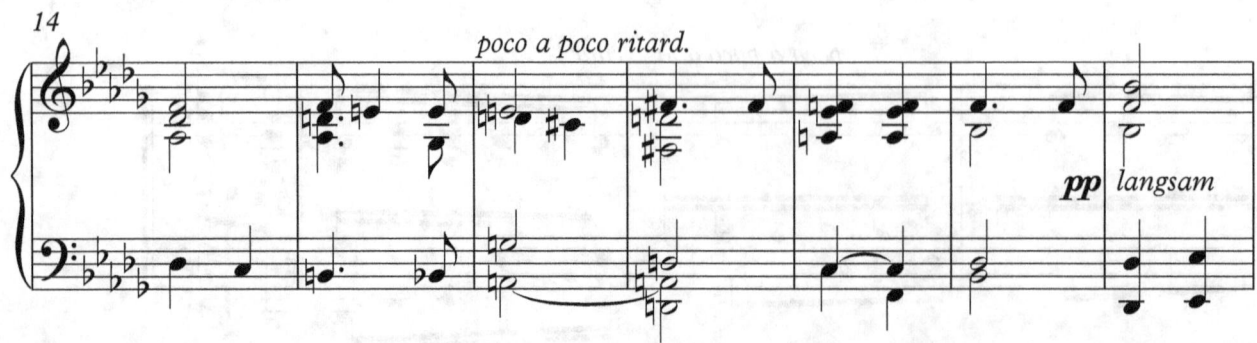

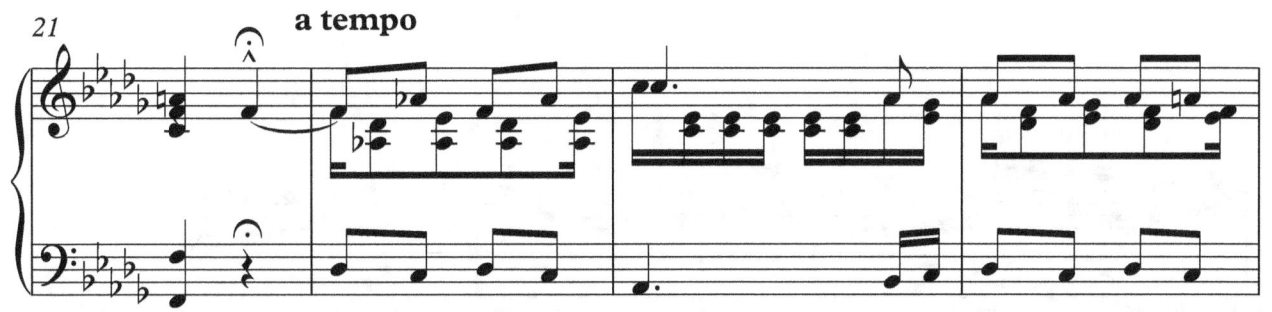

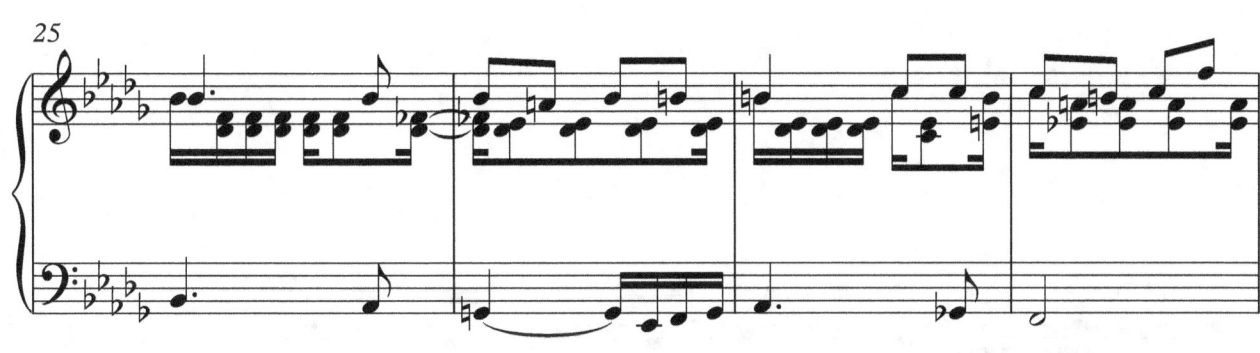

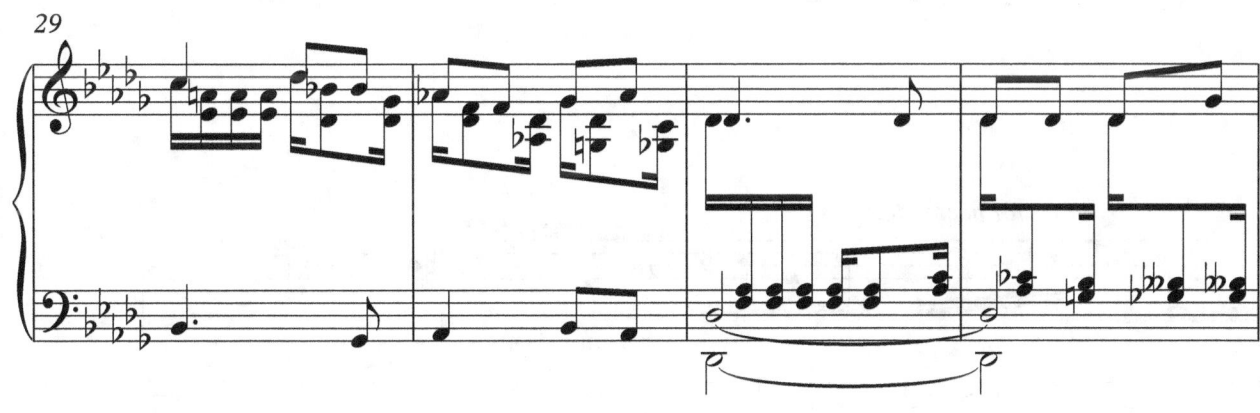

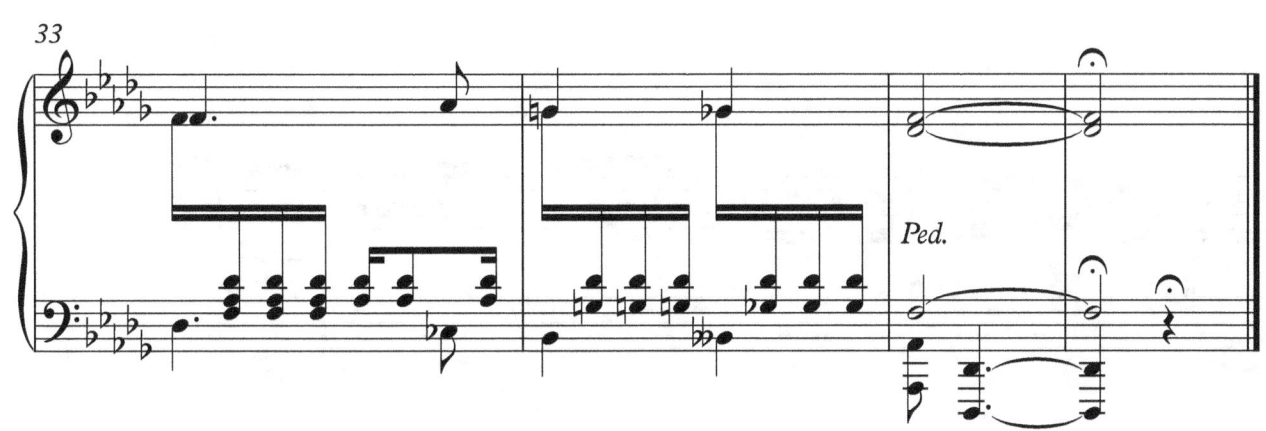

15. Two-part Prelude

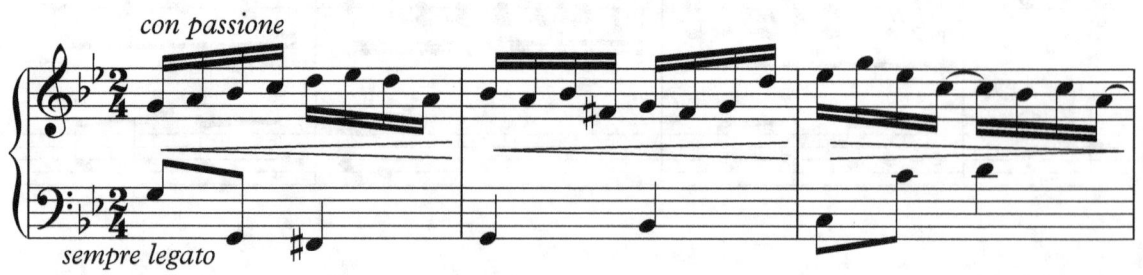

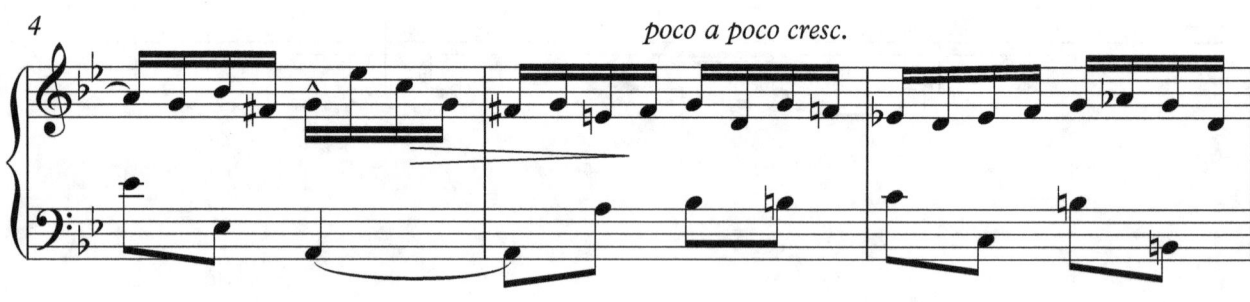

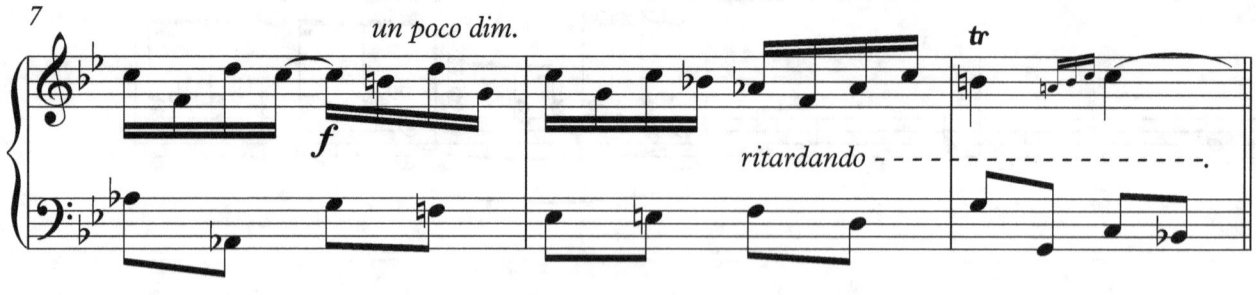

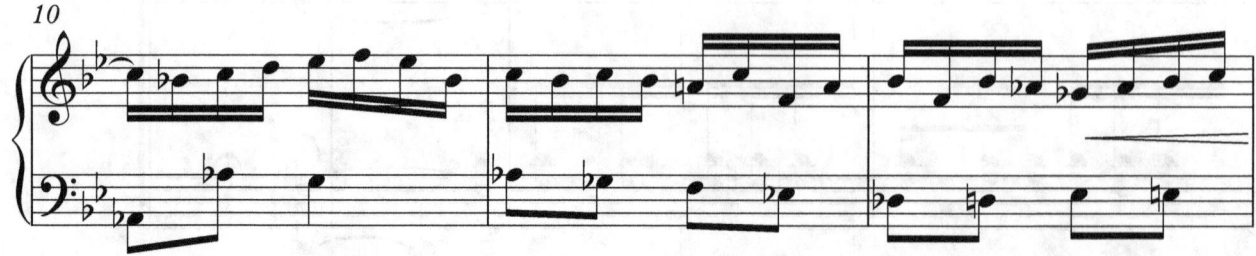

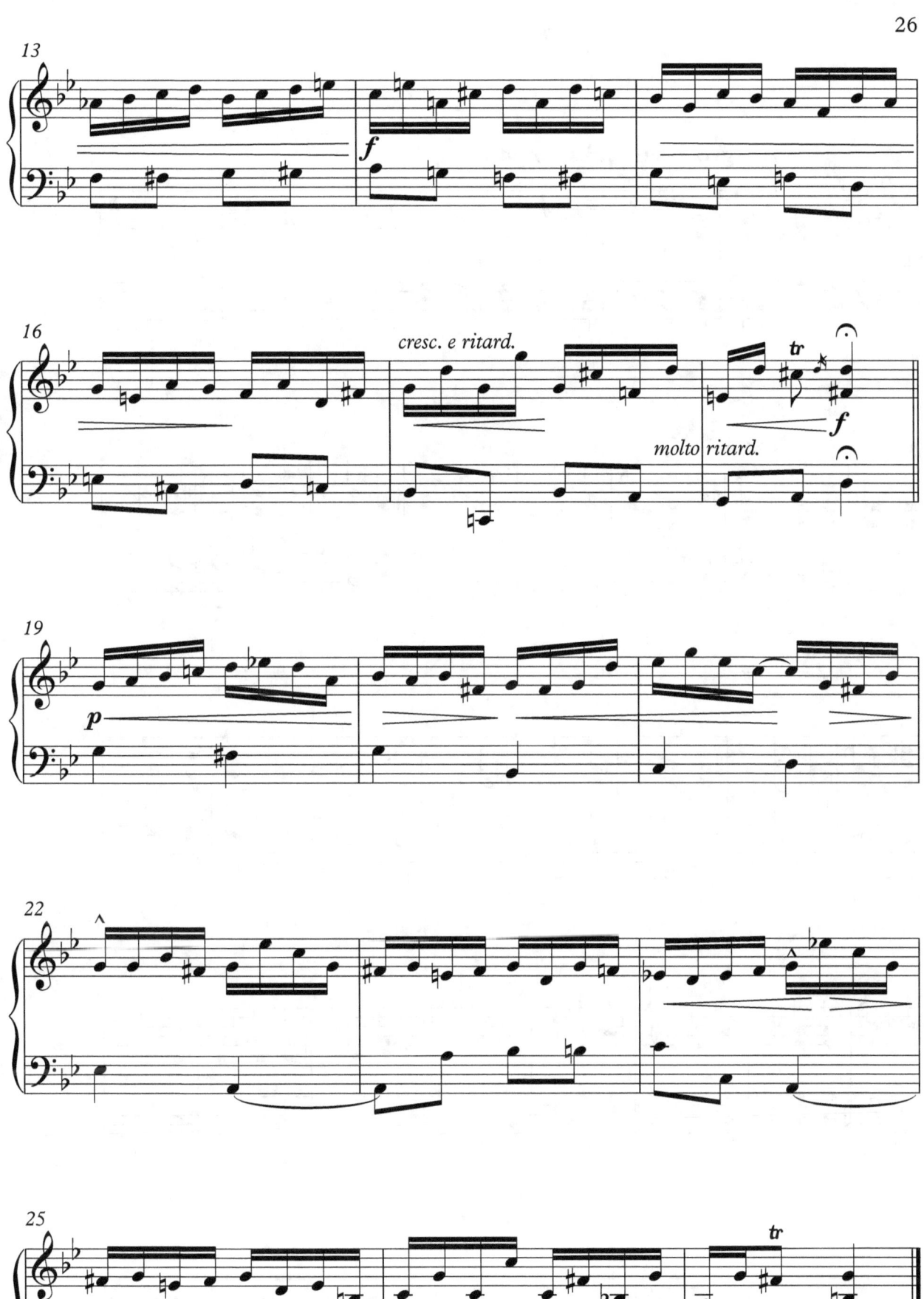

16.

Allegro assai, quasi presto

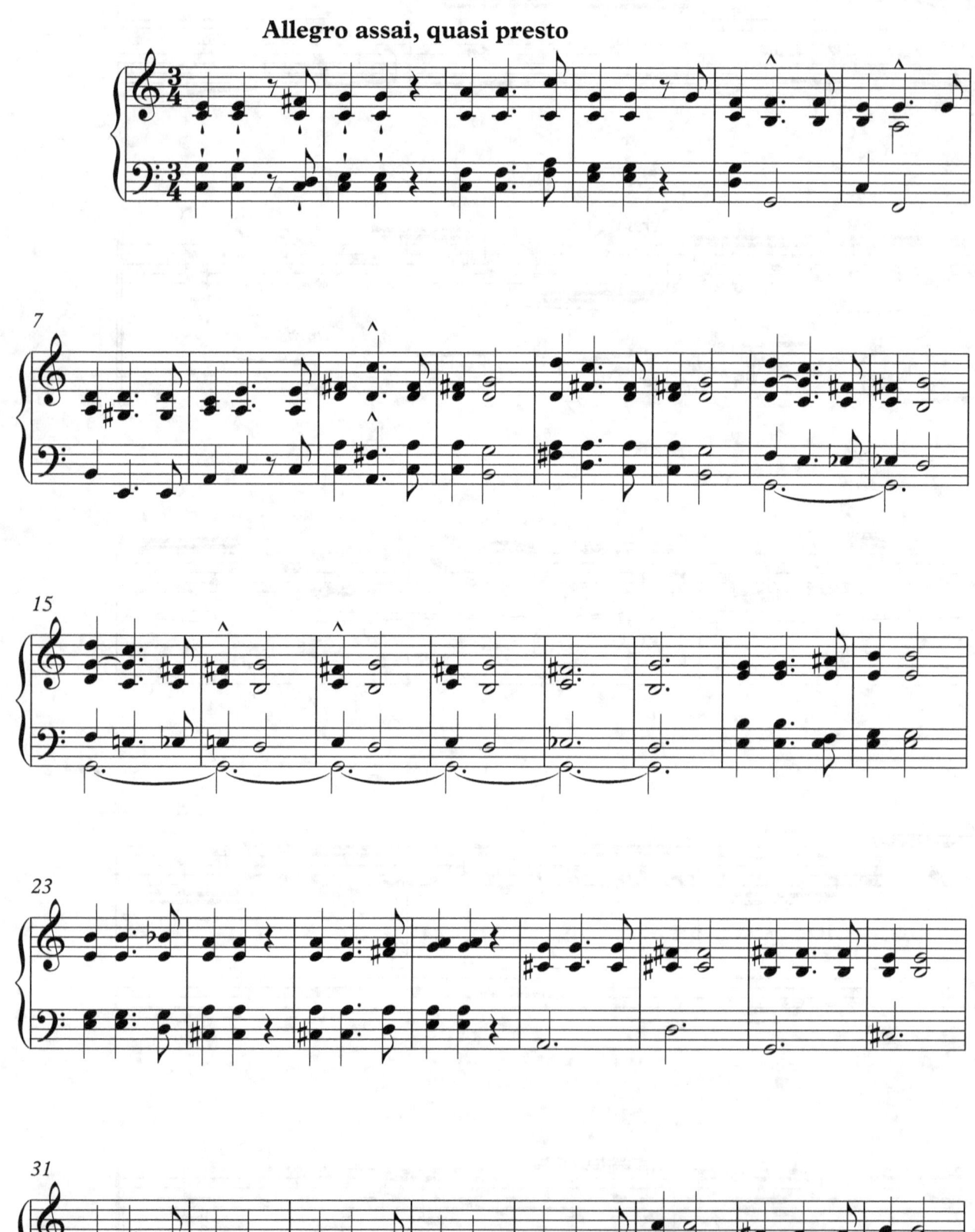

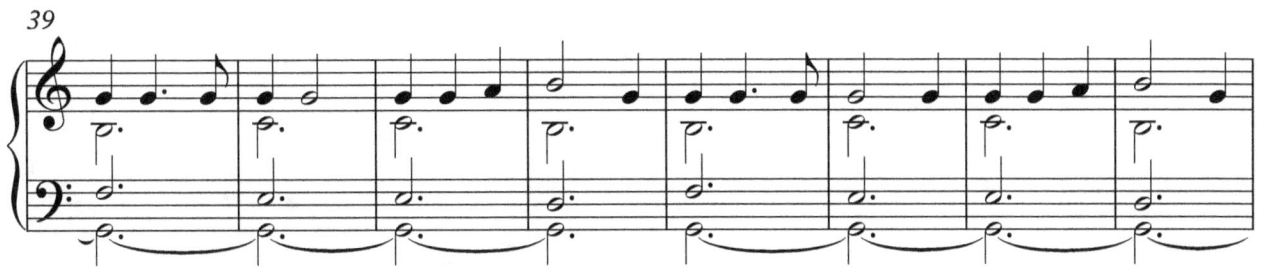

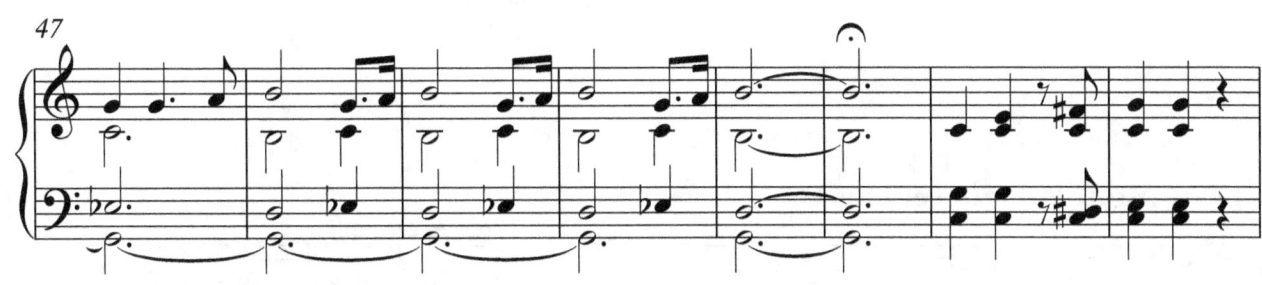

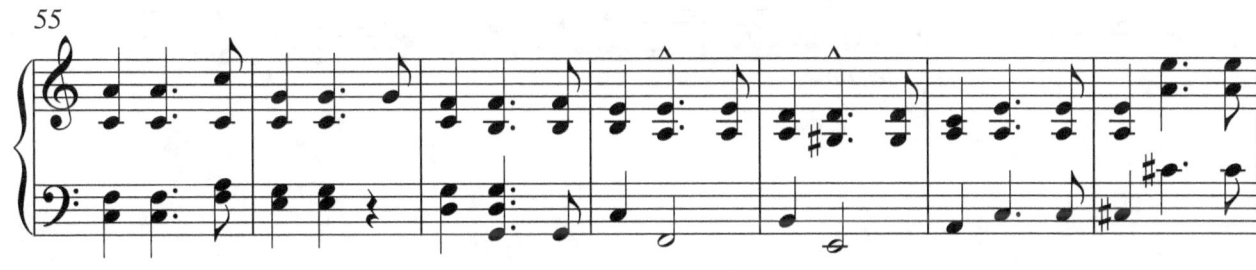

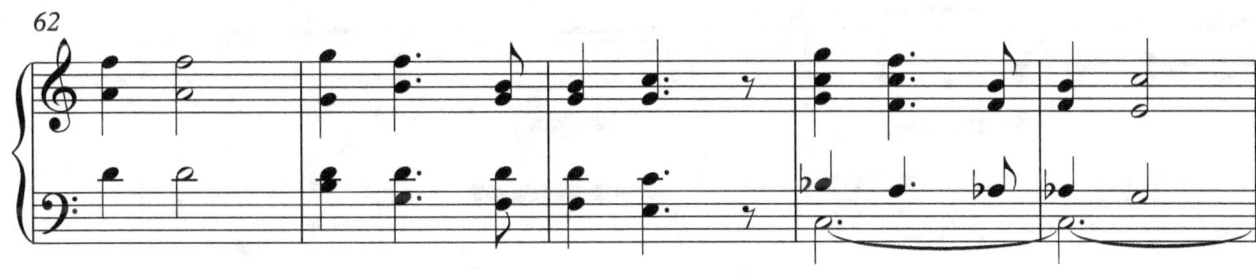

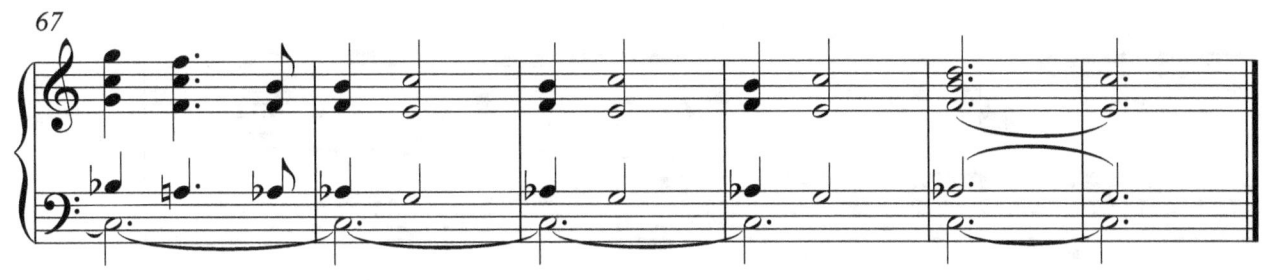

17.

1858

Molto Adagio religioso

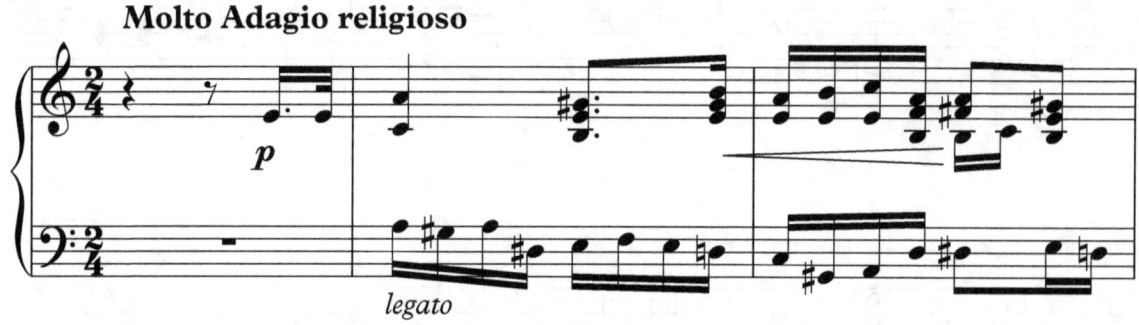

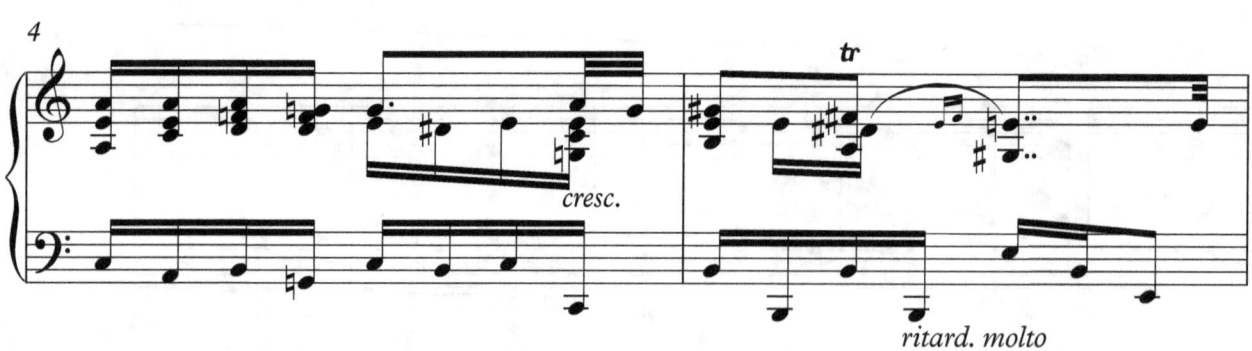

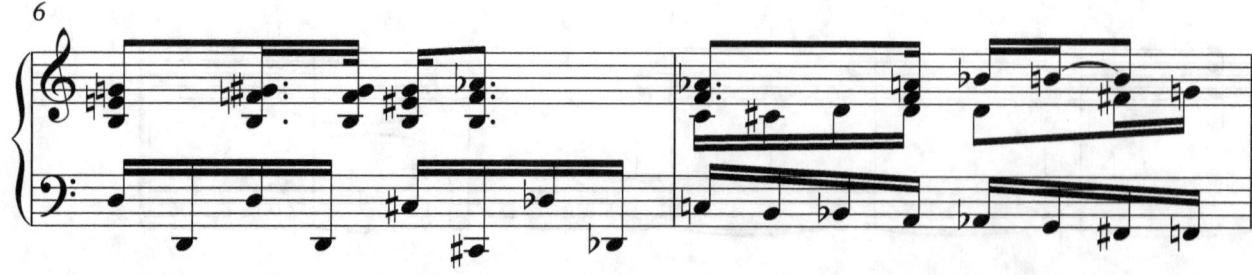

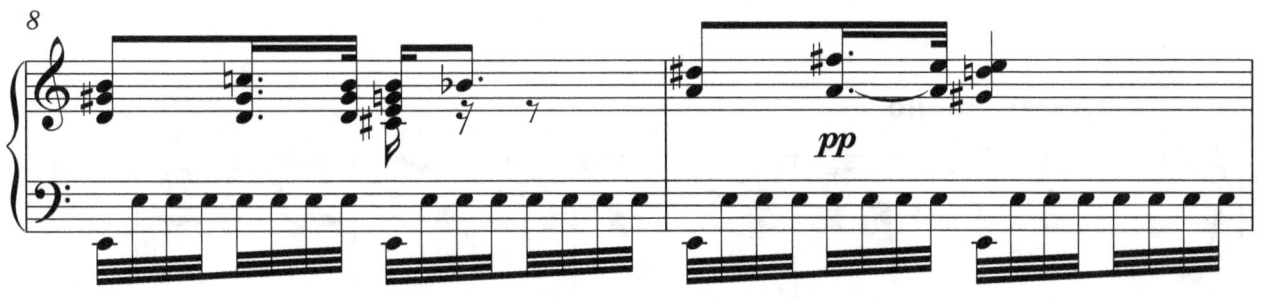

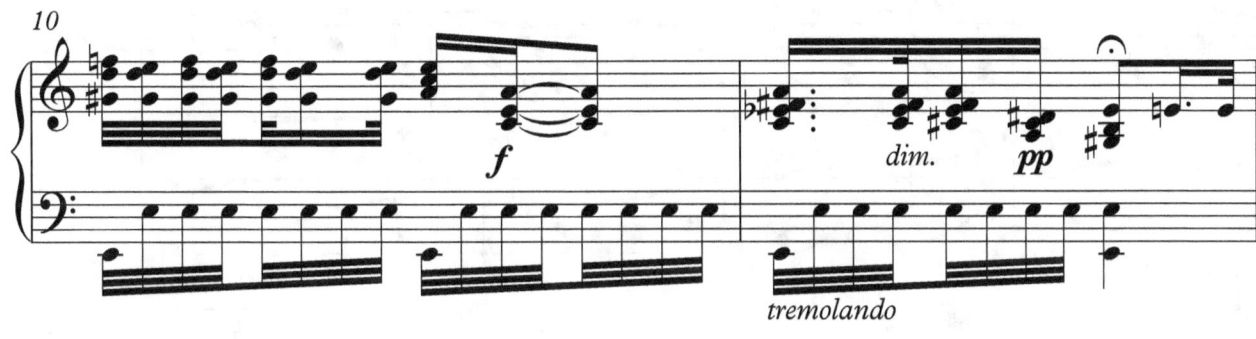

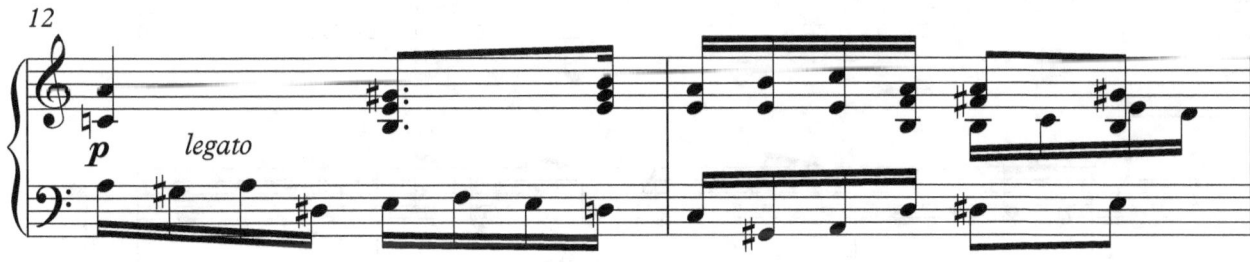

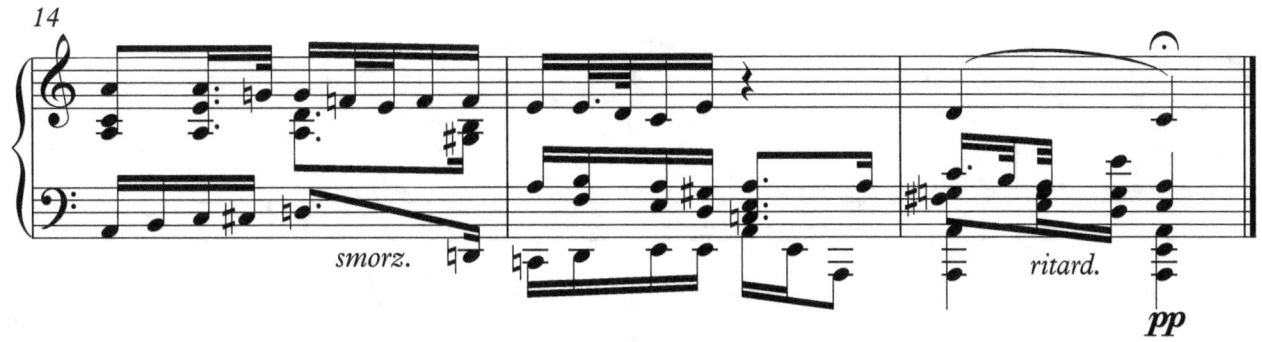

18.

Allegro molto

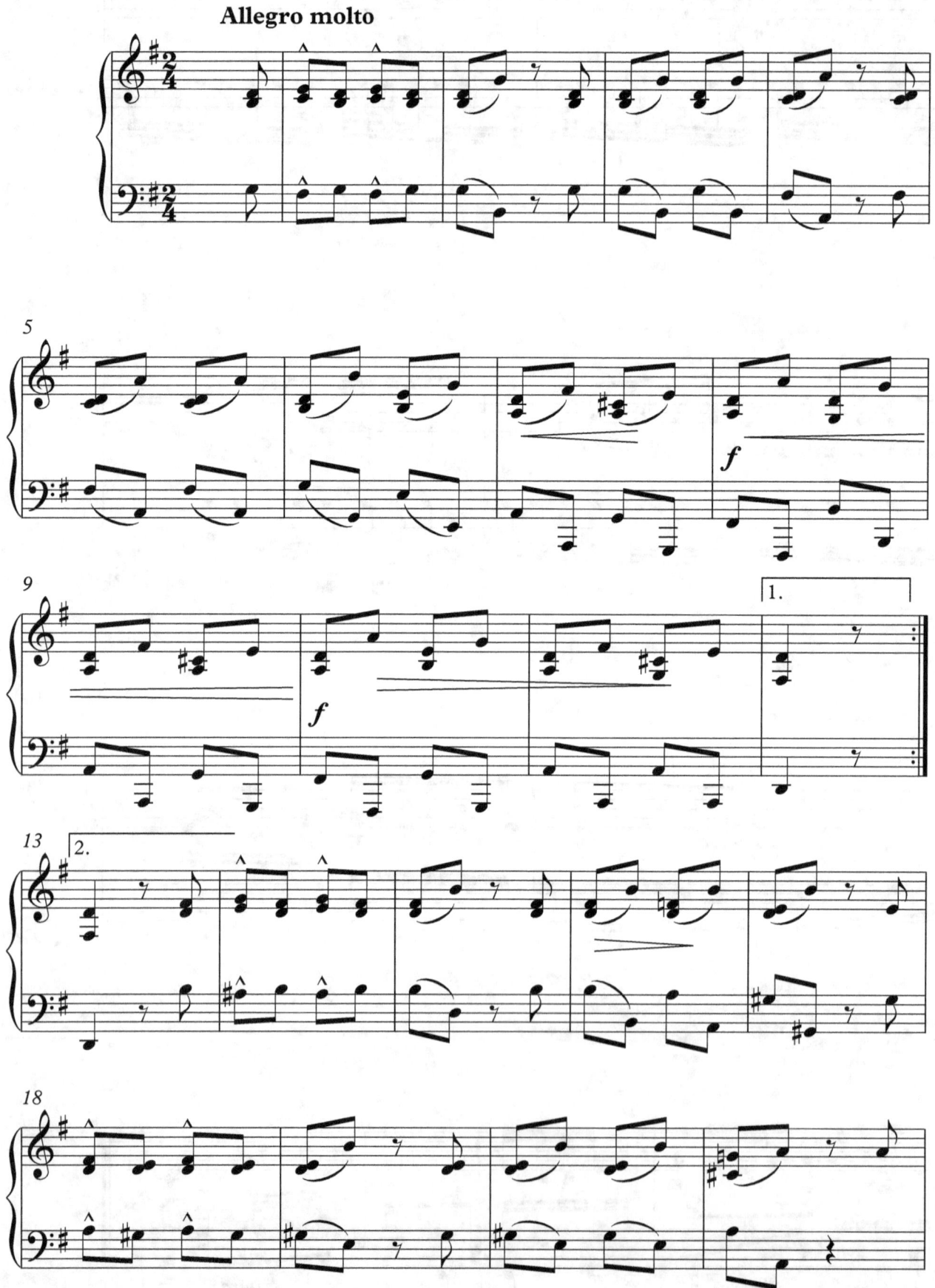

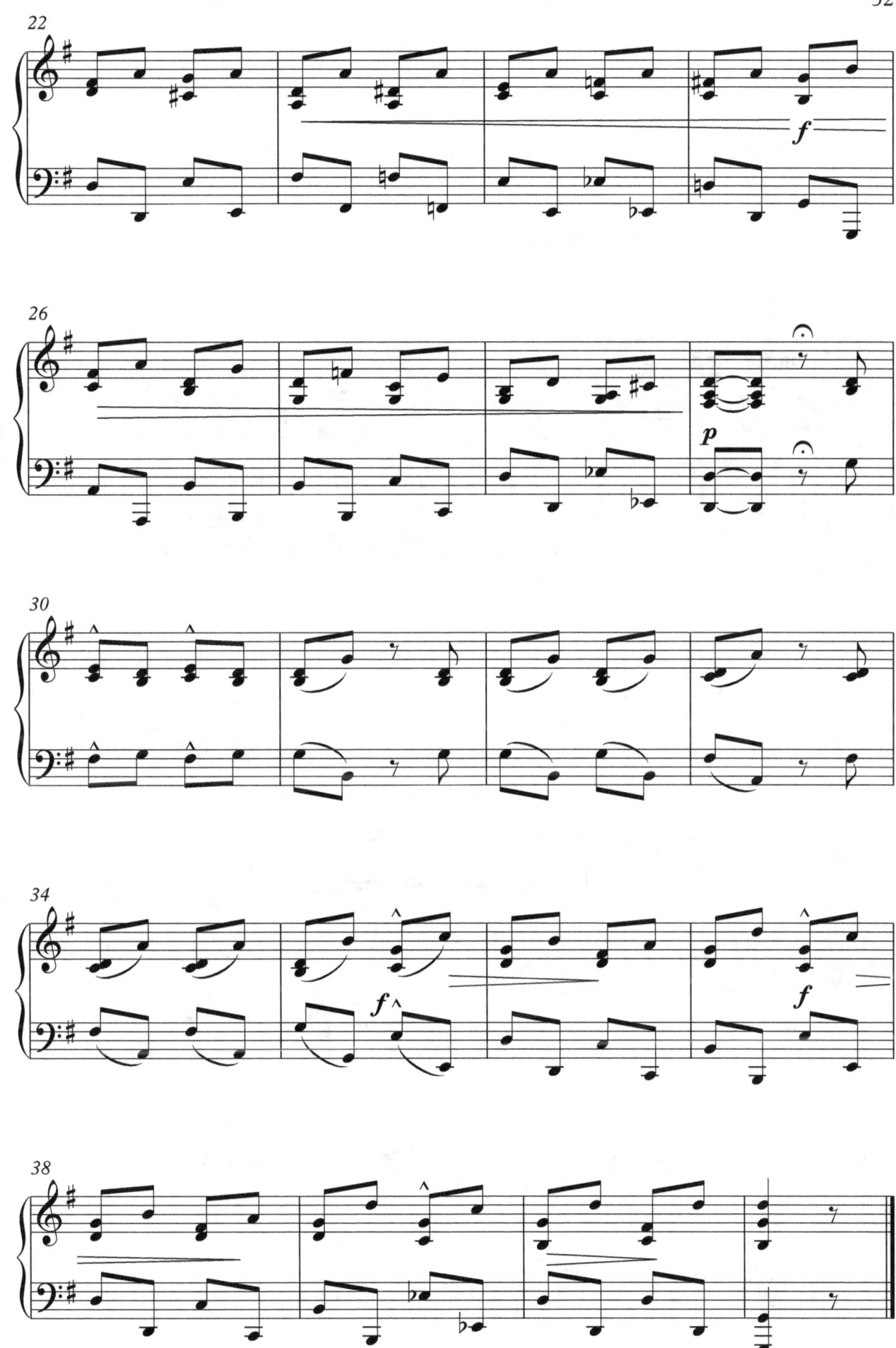

19.

Andante moderato

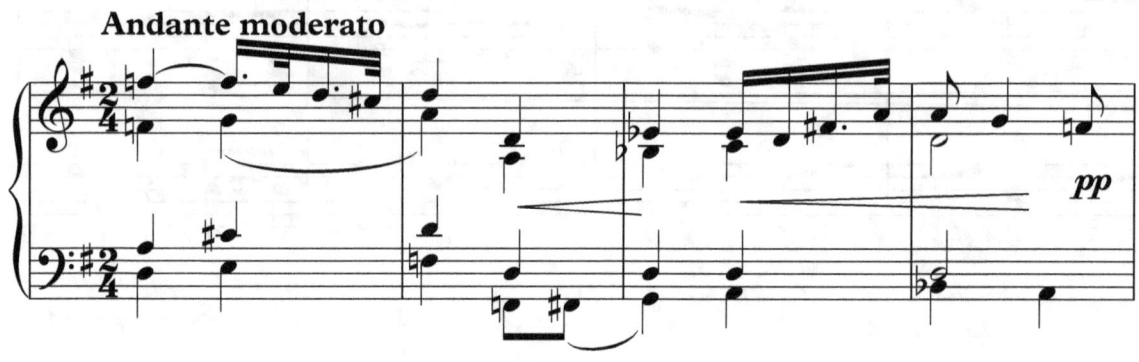

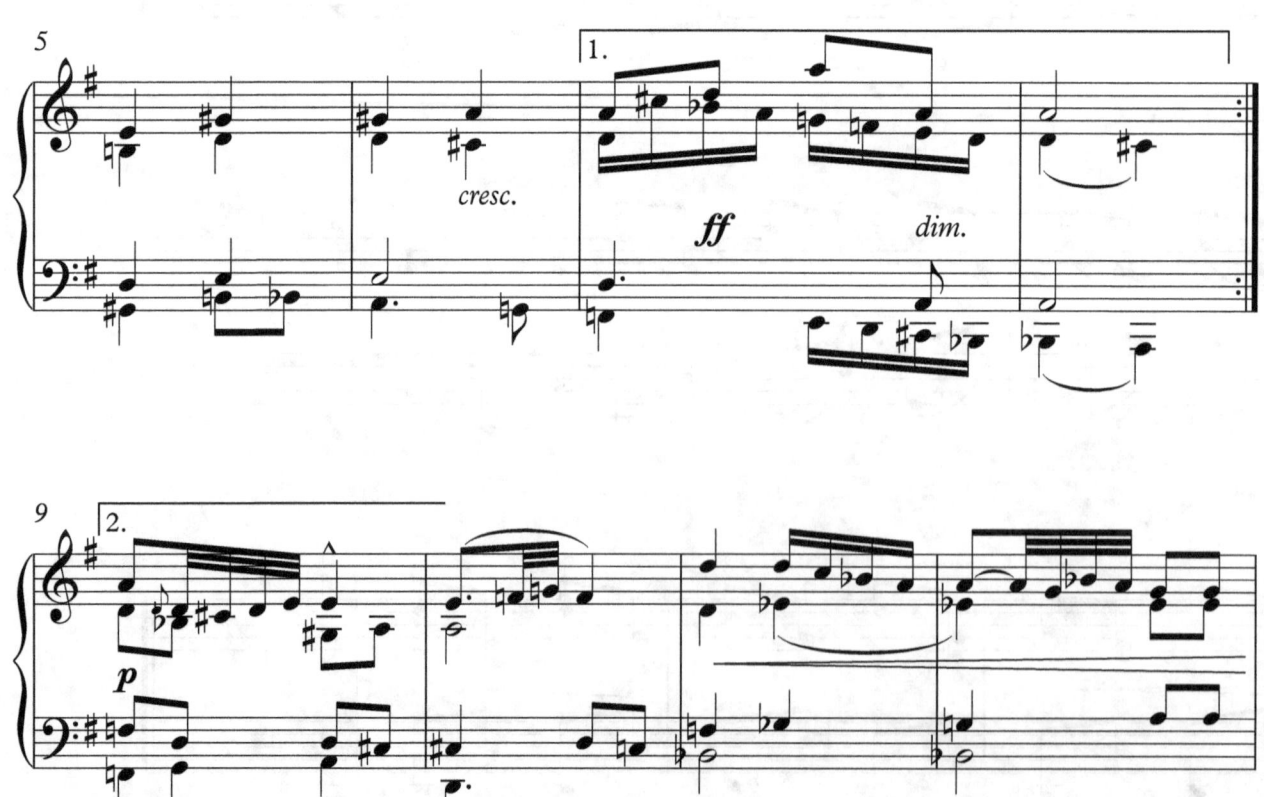

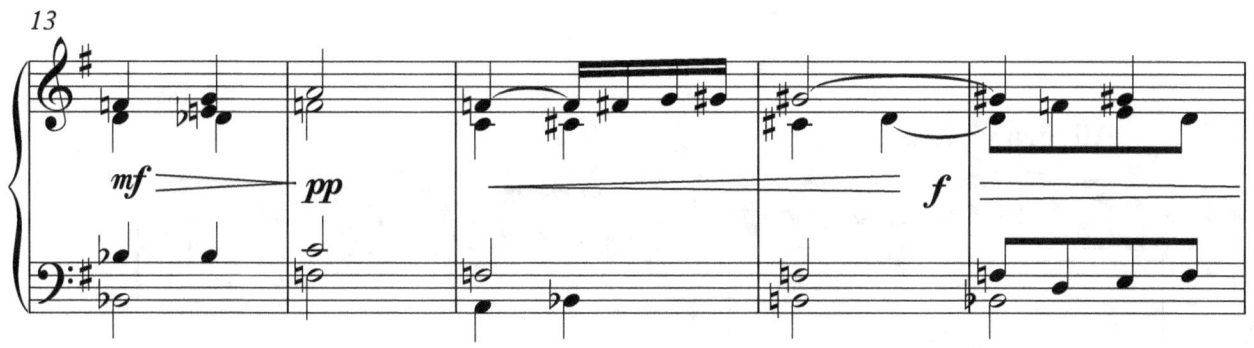

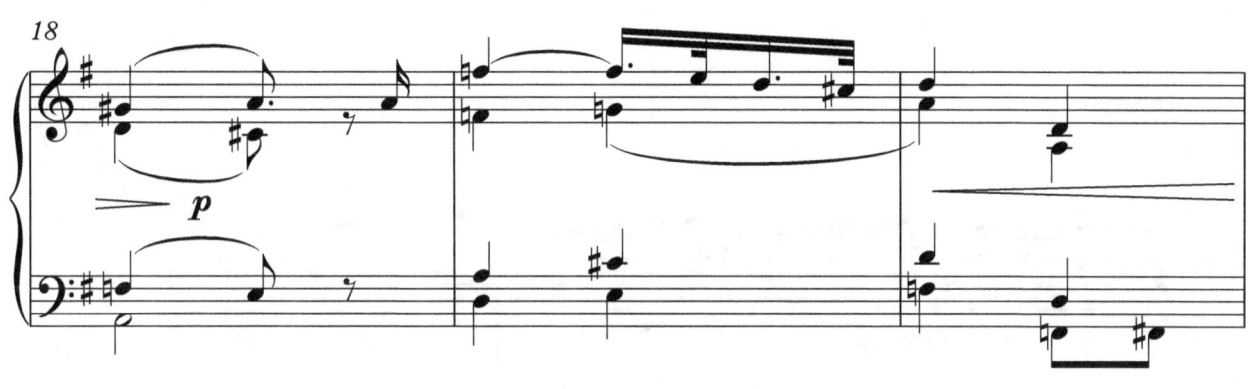

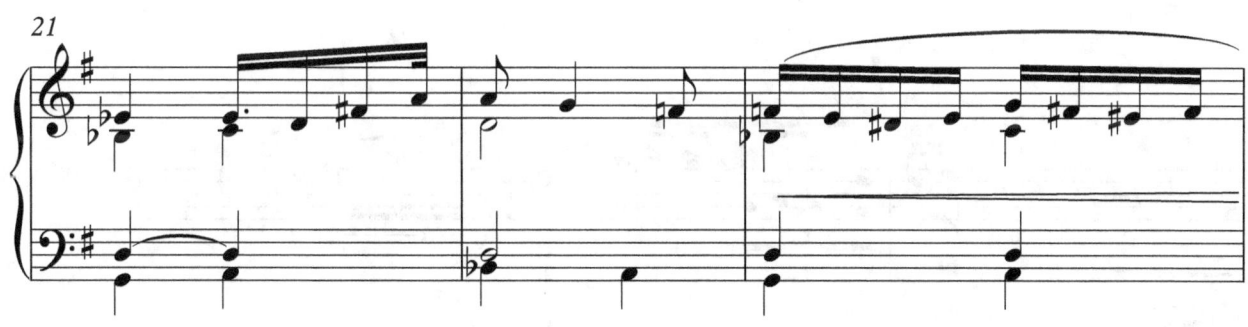

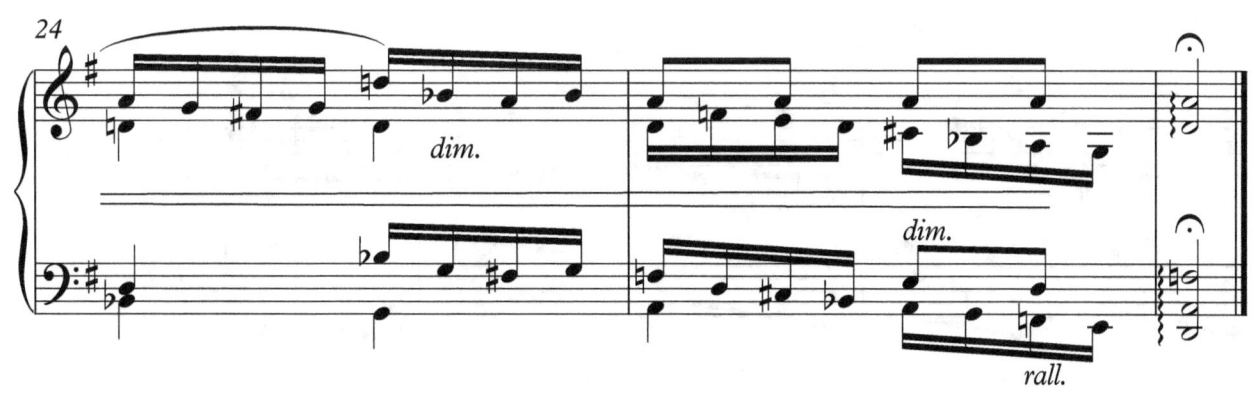

20.

1858

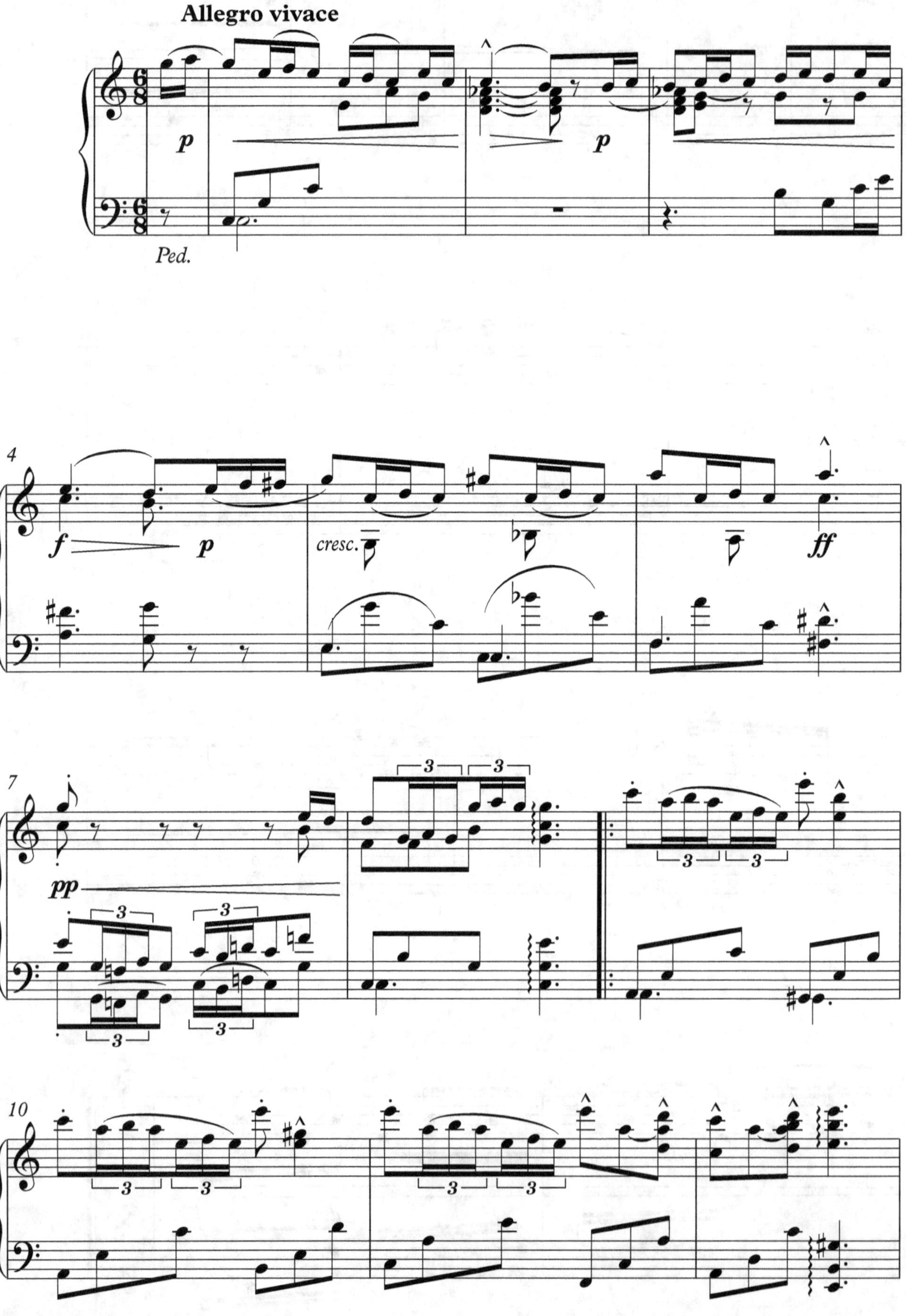

Allegro vivace

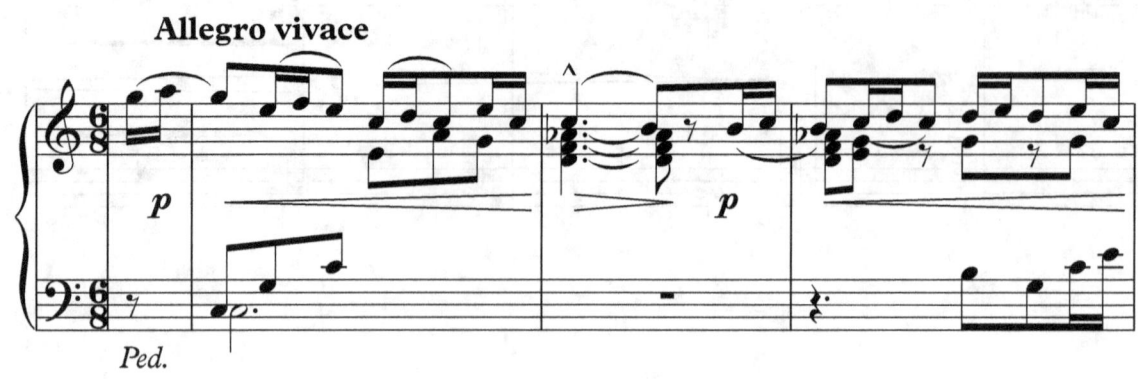

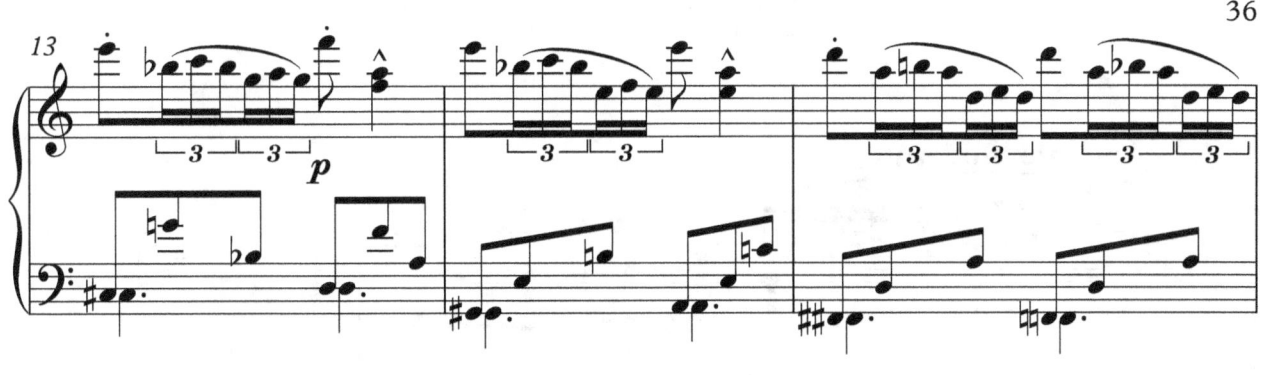

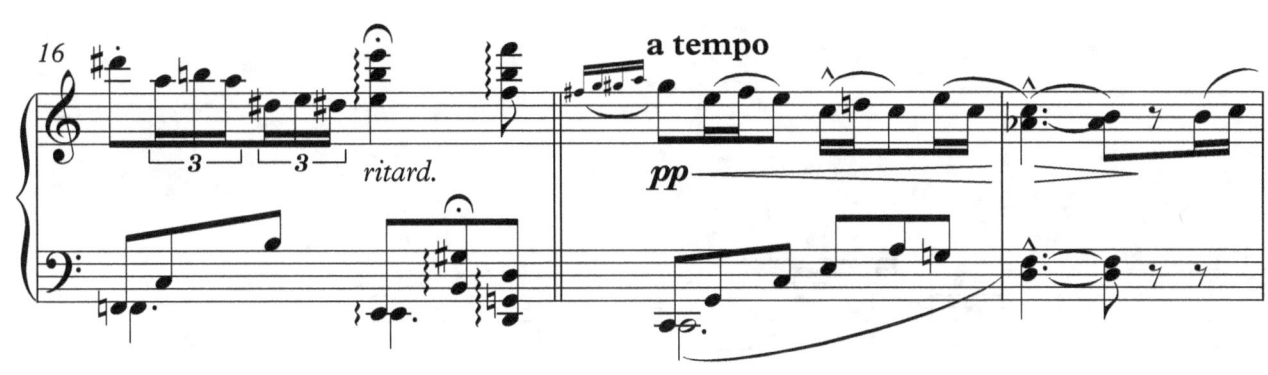

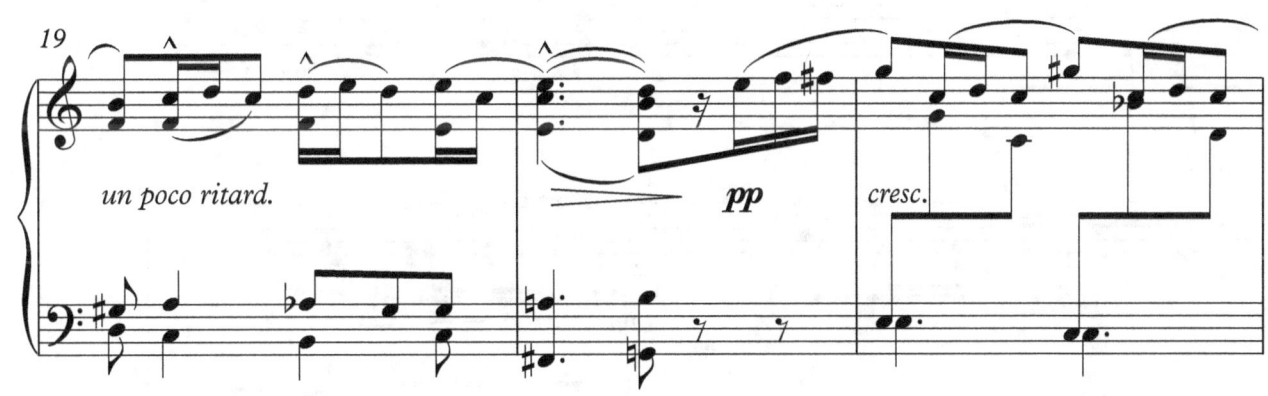

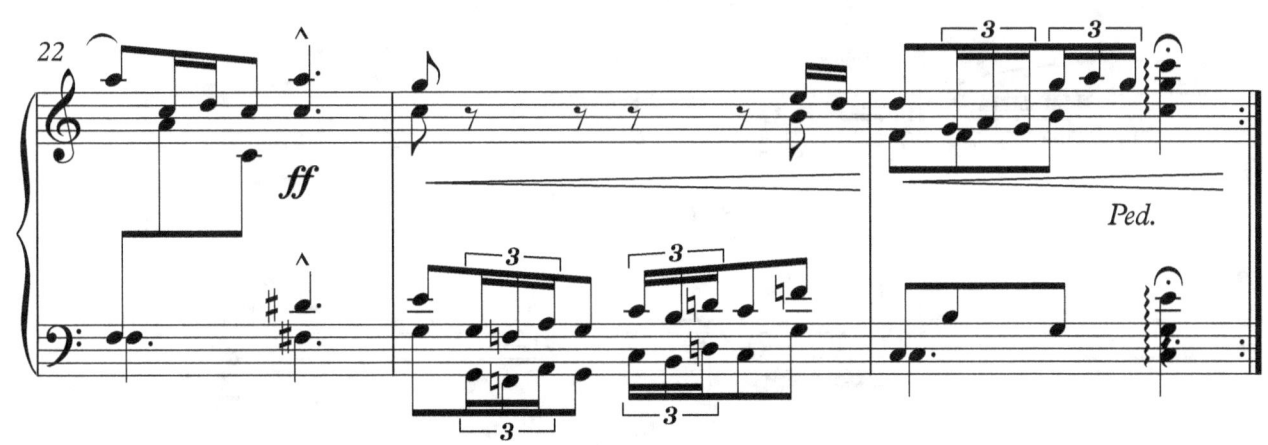

21.

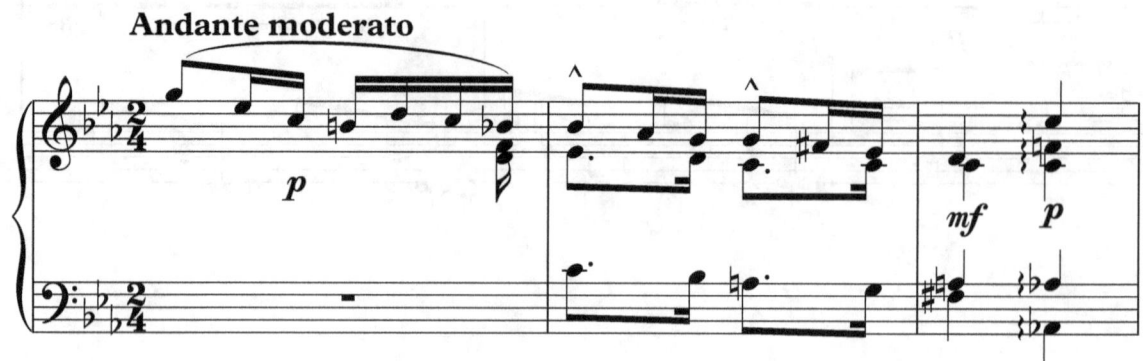

Andante moderato

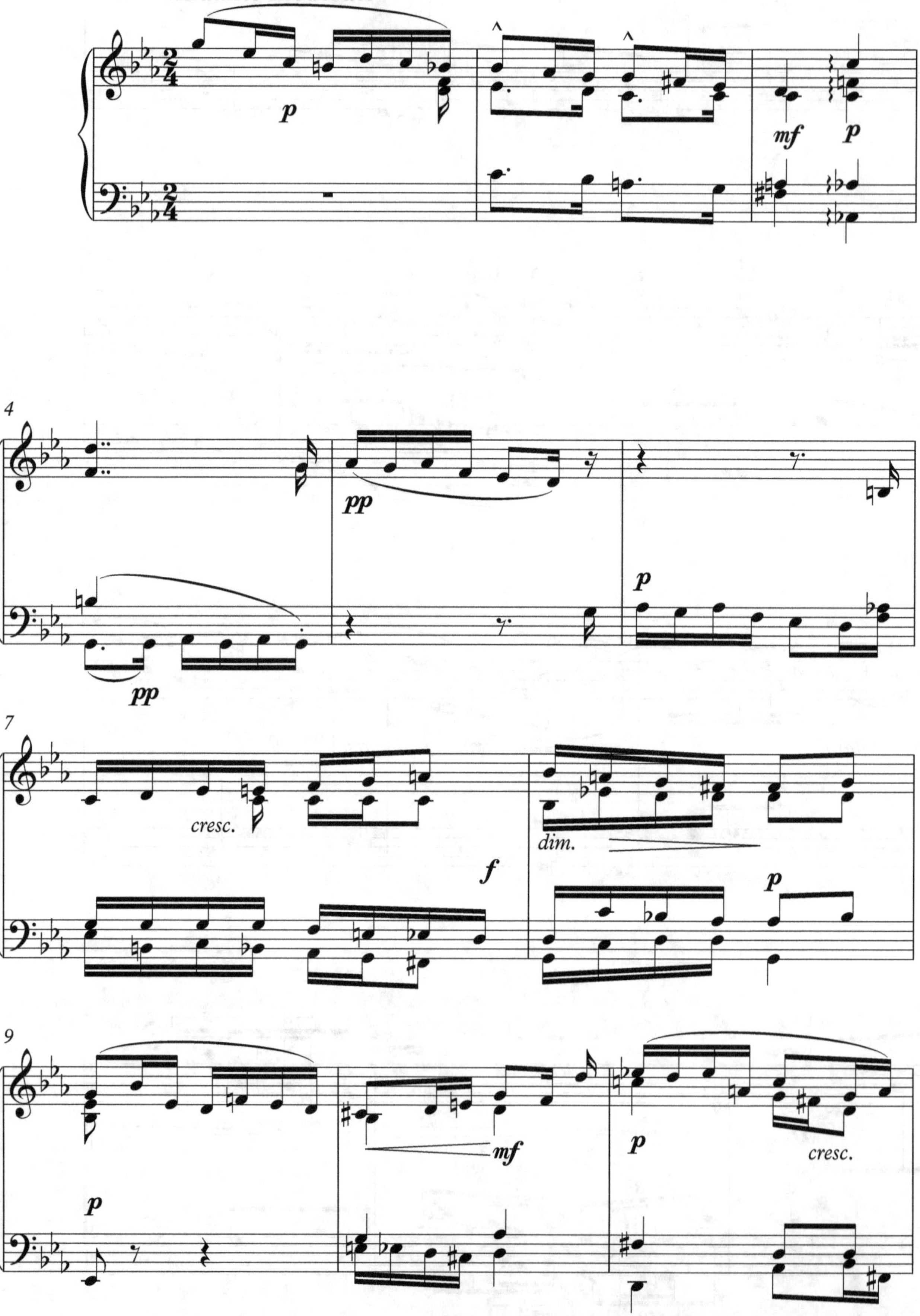

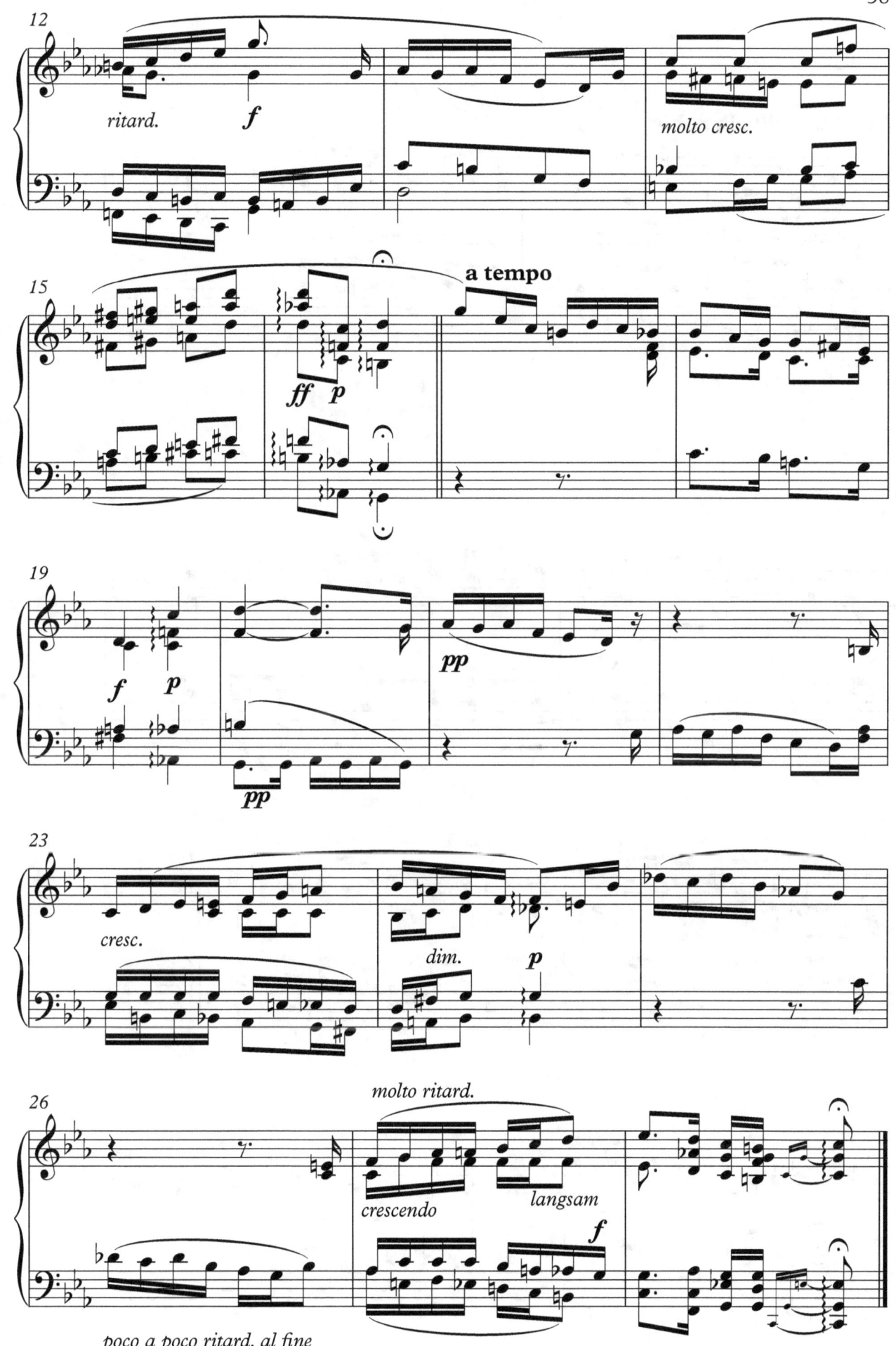

22.

Nicht zu schnell, ruhig

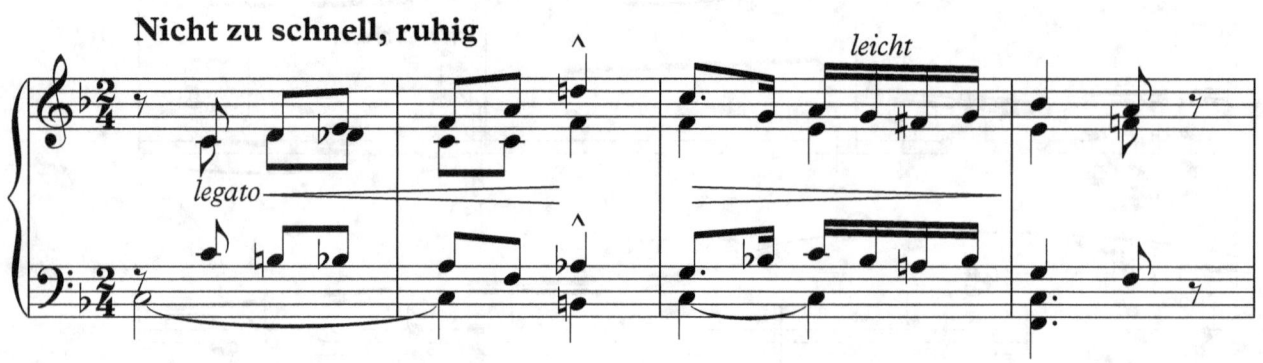

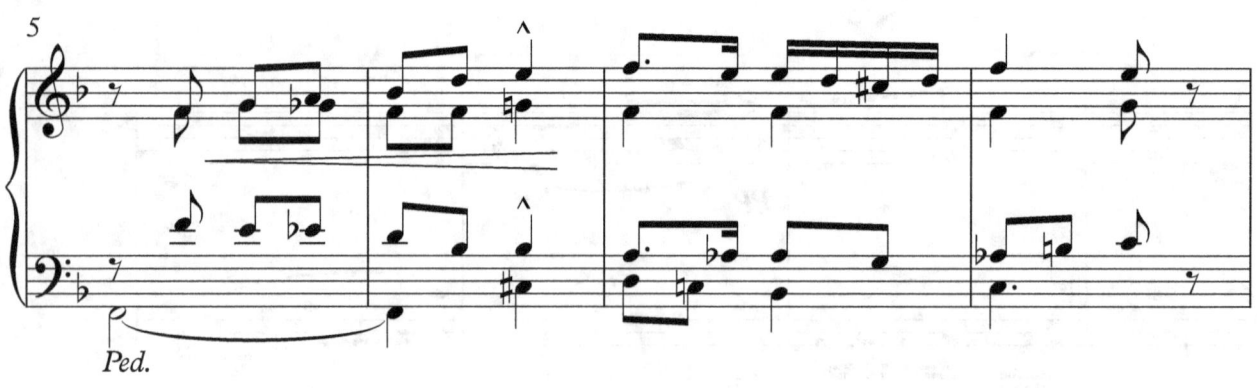

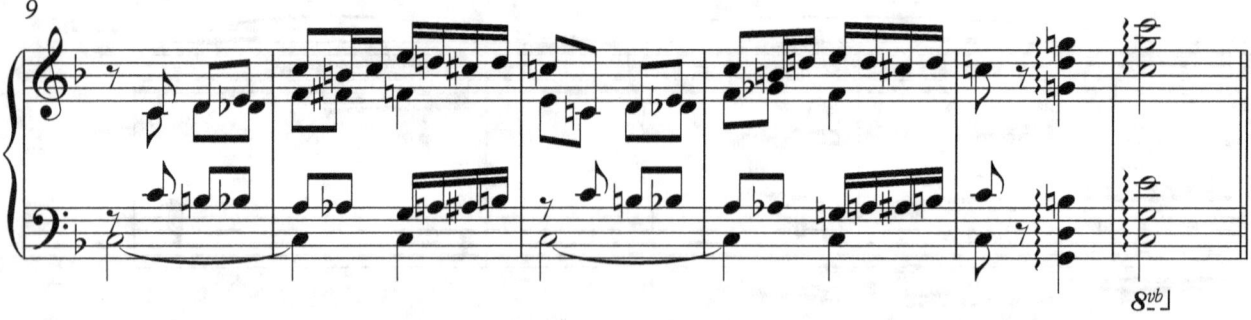

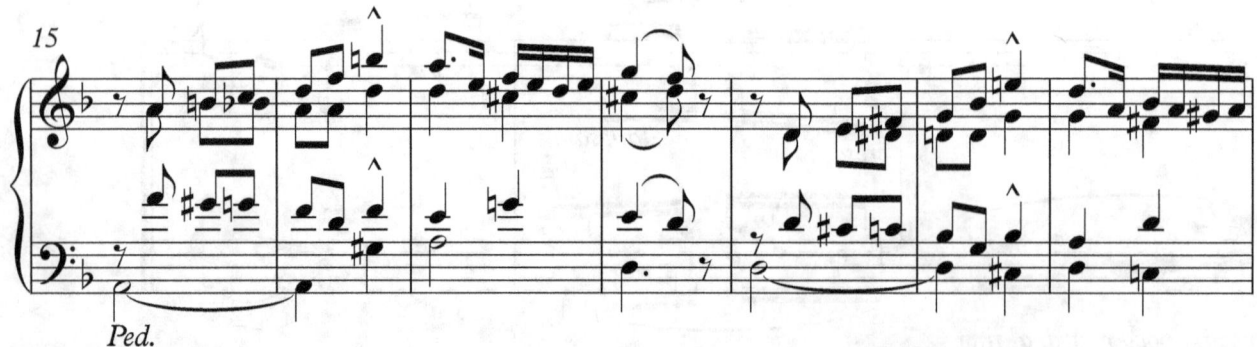

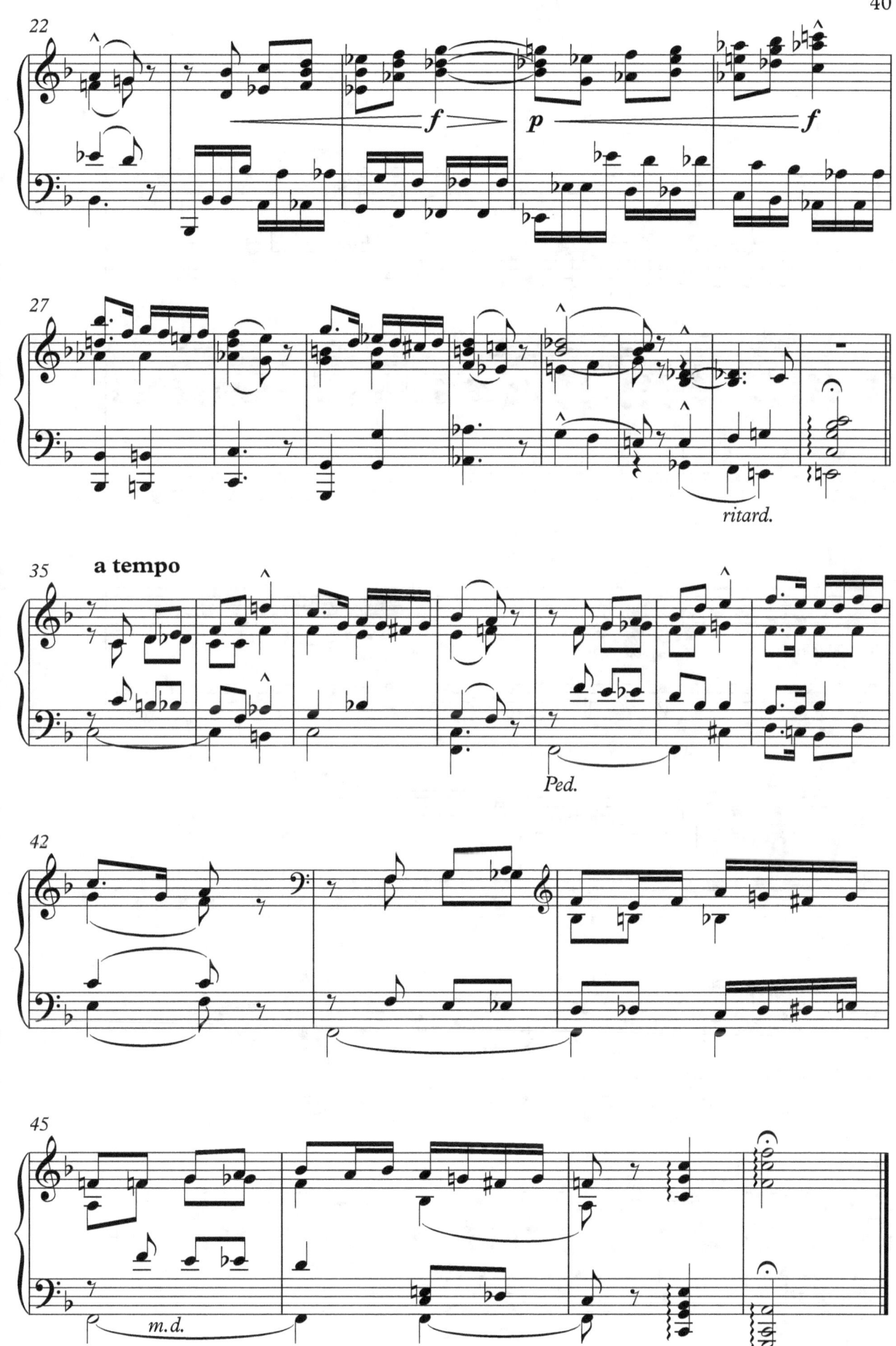

23.

Assai allegro furioso

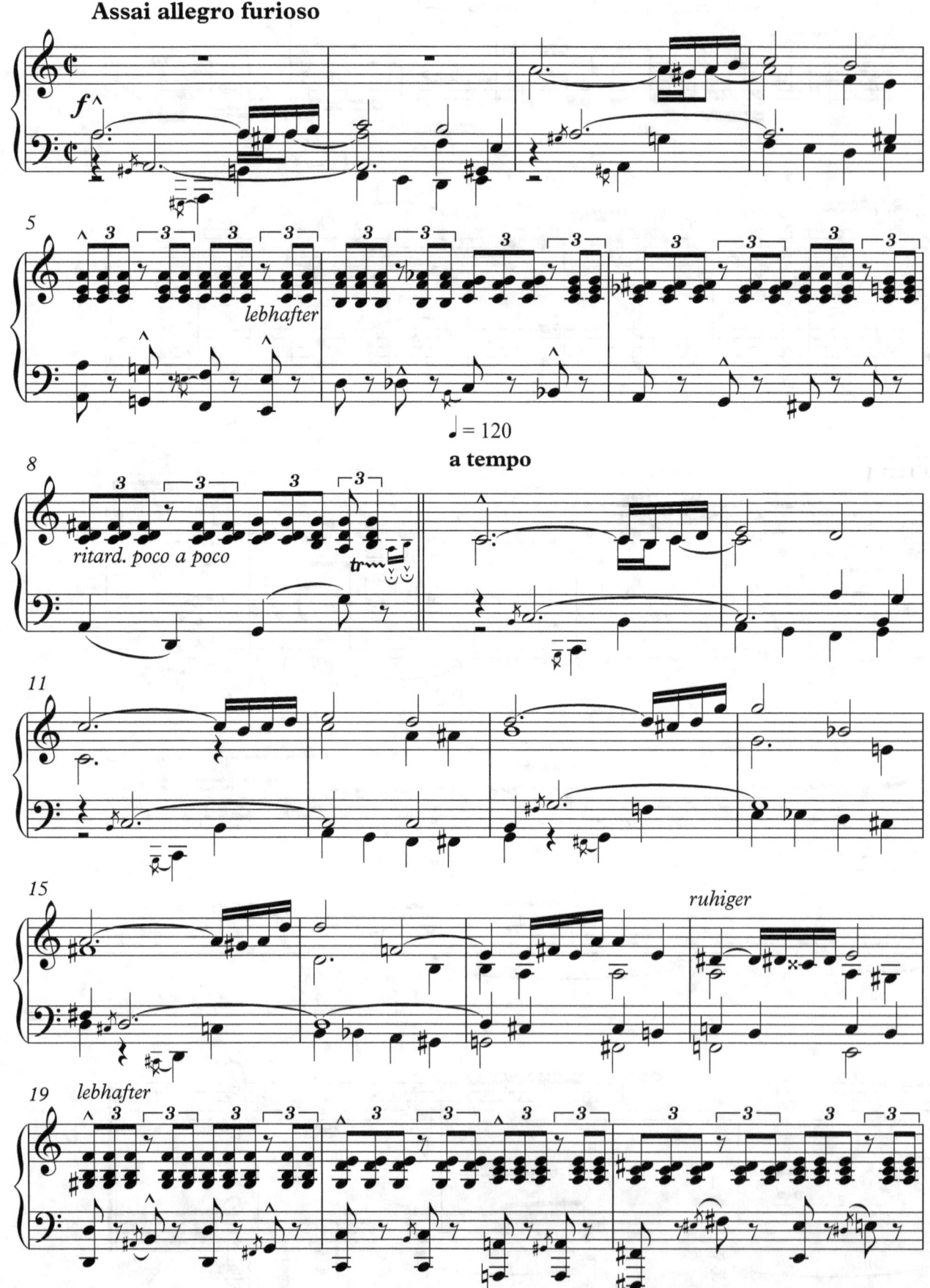

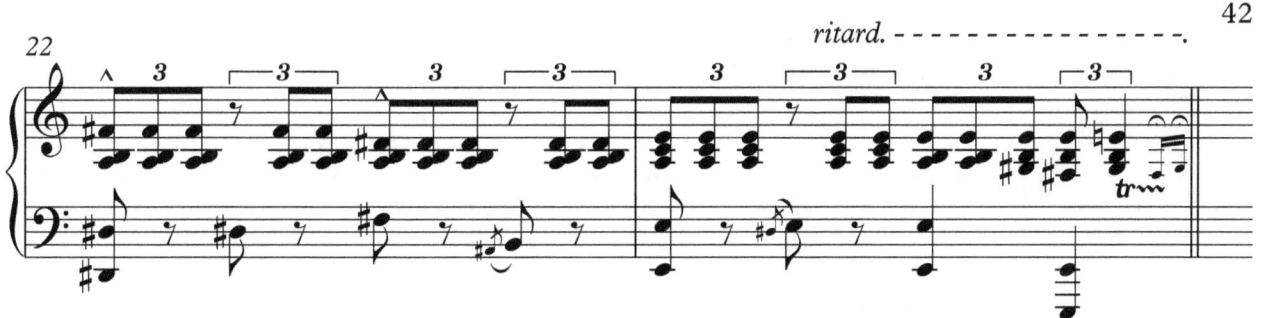

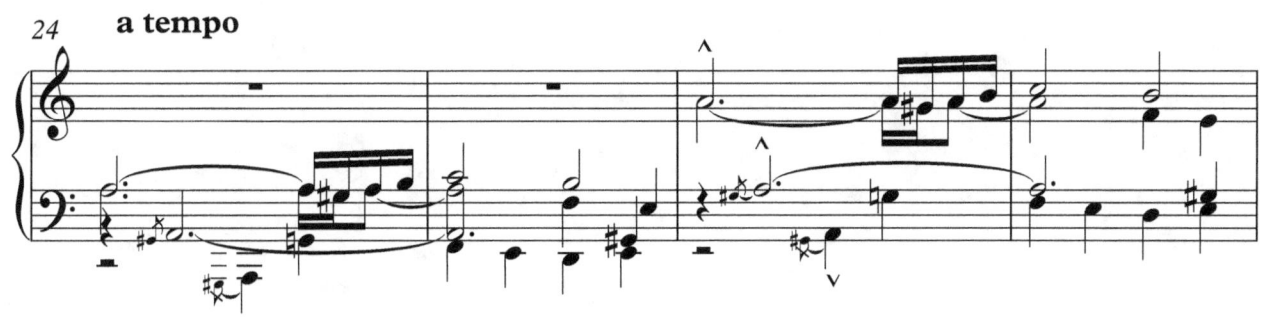

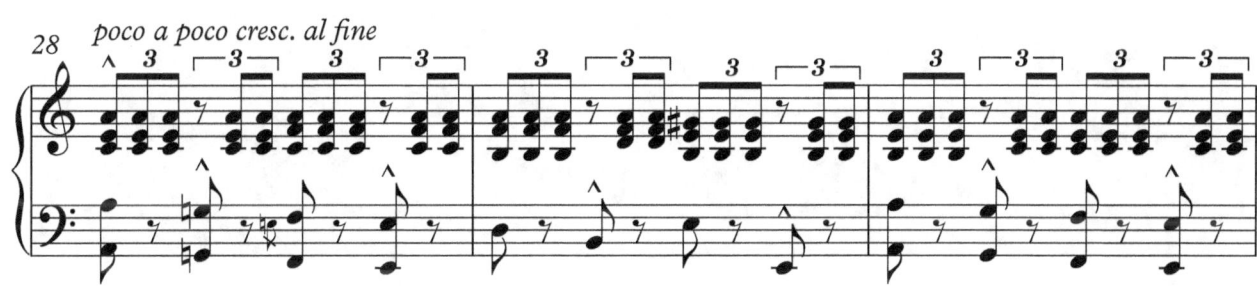

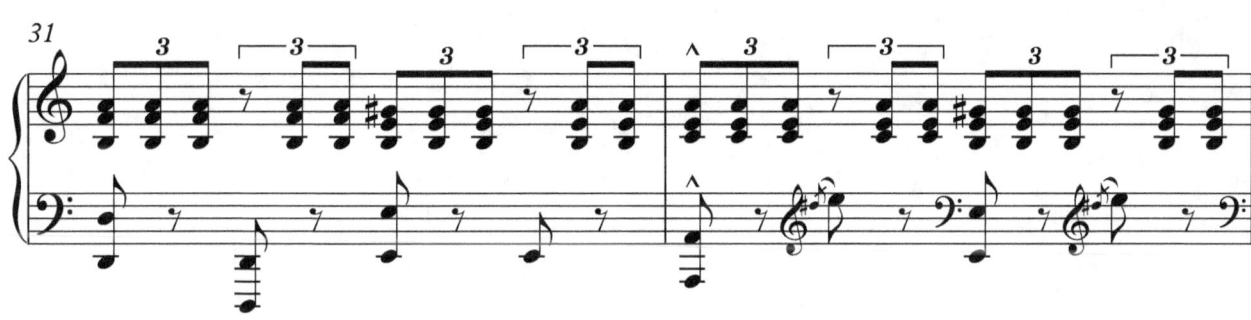

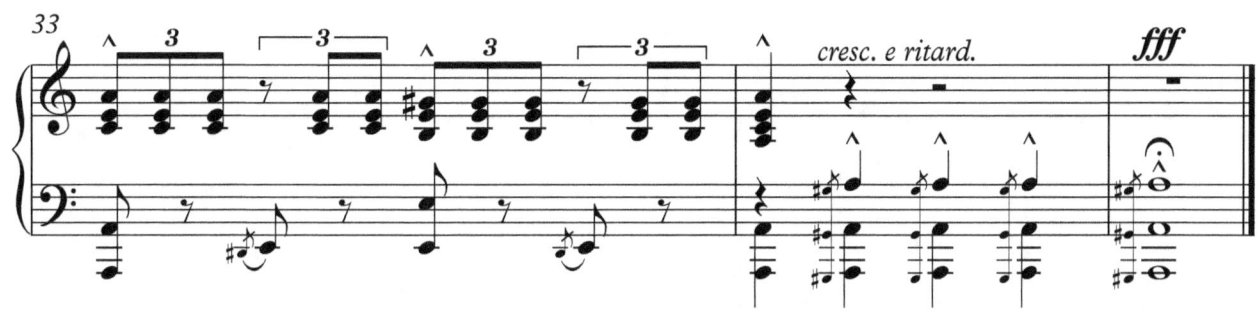